# GANGLAND MYSTERIES

# ESCOBAR VS CALI:
## THE WAR OF THE CARTELS

## RON CHEPESIUK

13-digit ISBN 978-1939-5210-1-9
10-digit ISBN 1-9395210-1-7

CONTENT

THE FEUD BETWEEN history's two most powerful drug trafficking cartels have been brewing for some time. The mutual hatred of drug kingpins such as Pablo Escobar and Helmer "Pacho" Herrera was the incendiary factor. In January 1988, Pablo Escobar was in firm control of the Medellin Cartel and still considered the world's greatest outlaw. Two years prior to that, the Colombian President, Virgilio Barco, had implemented the Colombian-US extradition treaty after the ruthless Escobar had launched vicious and violent campaigns that led to the deaths of hundreds of Colombian government officials and innocent Colombian citizens.

Pacho Herrera was one of the four founding members of the Cali Cartel, the rivals of the Medellin Cartel that had been steadily growing in wealth and power while Escobar took on the state. Herrera had returned to Cali, Colombia, from the U.S. in 1983 after a short prison term and he negotiated an arrangement with fellow Cali Cartel founders, the brothers Gilberto and Miguel Rodriguez Orejuela and Jose "Chepe." Santacruz Londono offered supply and distribution rights, which had allowed him to build a base in New York City. In recognition of his value to the Cali cartel, Herrera was made a member of its "board of directors," and he proved invaluable to his associates by using his contacts to help open up Mexico.

Pablo Escobar was arrogant and a bully, while Herrera was stubborn and tough. They came to hate each other over what would seem like a trivial matter: a dispute over a worker for one of Escobar's New York distributors. While in prison during the early 1980s, Herrera had befriended a Colombian named Pina, a worker for Jaime Pabon, who was a major cocaine distributor for Escobar. But Pina angered Pabon when he philandered with a member of Pabon's family, and he had to flee. Pina sought support from the Herrera organization.

At first, Pacho Herrera balked at hiring Pina because he knew Pabon was a close associate of the powerful and violent Escobar. He did not need to rile El Patron, or The Boss, as Escobar was known.

That did not satisfy Pabon, though, who was going unhappy until he had Pina killed for dishonoring his family. He asked Escobar for help. No problem. Escobar figured that a single call to Chepe Santacruz to complain about

Pacho Herrera's protection of Pina, would be enough to persuade him and the other Cali bosses to use their influences on Herrera and get him to turn Pina over to Pabon.

The Rodriguez brothers, Pacho Herrera and Santacruz had a meeting. They knew the consequences of defying Pablo, but they decided that maintaining a united front was the best response to his intimidating threat. "We have no quarrel with Pina," was their terse reply to Escobar.

Pina would not let the matter go. He lied to Escobar. "The Cali cartel plans to kidnap you," Pina told Escobar. The enraged Escobar called Herrera and demanded that Pina give up Pabon within 24 hours or he would kill Herrera's entire family. Rather than being intimidated, Herrera took Escobar's demand as a slight to his honor. There are times in the cutthroat world of drug trafficking when honor takes precedence over business. Herrera called his brother Ramon, who was managing his cell in New York City, and ordered him to hire Pina immediately.

Gilberto Rodrigues Orejuela tried to cool things down by personally contacting Escobar and trying to convince him that their two respective organizations should not go to war over such a trivial matter as the fate of a low-level worker in Queens, New York. But both sides would not back down.

The cities of Cali and Medellin were a mere 100 miles part and it seemed unthinkable—and indeed foolhardy— for drug traffickers, no matter how powerful they are in their own rights, to challenge Escobar. The Boss felt secured in his magnificent eight-story apartment building in Medellin. Known as Edificio Monaco, the building had paintings by Botero, Picasso and other masters worth millions and floors made of imported marbles. Made of reinforced steel, Edificio Monaco also had the first security cameras system in Colombia. It also had an underground bunker and a roof top helicopter pad where armed guards stood ready to whisk Escobar away in case of an attack by the authorities or his enemies.

The Cali Cartel godfathers tried to kill El Patron by sending Andes "Freckles" Velez, one of their most loyal soldiers to Medellin with a carload of dynamite. Velez had reportedly killed one of his own brothers for betraying the Cali Cartel. Velez parked his car beneath the Monaco building, expecting Escobar and his family to be sleeping in the penthouse. But on this particular night, after Escobar had dinner with his family, Escobar decided to go to his farm, which was located about ten miles from Medellin. A powerful blast shook Medellin. The bomb was so powerful that most city residents heard it when it went off.

The explosion killed two security guards, wounded several people and left a crater 12-feet deep and twenty-one feet across the outside of the apartment building. Miraculously, Escobar's wife Maria and their two children survived, although the explosion partially deafened their infant daughter, Manuela, who was sleeping in a crib.

Two right-wing groups immediately claimed responsibility for the attack, declaring that their intent was to rid Medellin of criminals and drug traffickers. But The Patron had no doubt who was behind the attack. Gilberto Rodriguez Orejuela had called Escobar about half an hour after the bombing.

"I heard about the bombing, Pablo," Gilberto said. "Are you okay?"

Escobar played dumb, but he was already thinking how he could exact revenge. He had long suspected that his rivals could not be trusted.

In the wake of the attack, Escobar sent sicarios, or hit men, to Cali to find his enemies and kill them. Figuring that the best defense was a good offense, the Cali godfathers sent hit men to Medellin.

The war of the cartels was on.

# CHAPTER ONE

# THE RISE OF EL PATRON

N THE MID 1990s, no one could have imagined a gang war in Colombia that threatened the security of the state and terrorized its populace. At that time, drug traffickers were shipping a few hundred kilos of cocaine at a time, not the multi-ton shipments that would become common by the 1980s. The cocaine kingpins of the mid-1970s relied not on ships, boats and trucks but on "mules" – individuals who carried drugs into the United States in hollowed-out platform shoes, double-bottomed suitcases, stuffed animals or various containers. The cocaine was hermetically sealed in plastic bags and normally packed in half-kilogram units. The mules were usually Colombians recruited while applying for visas to enter the United States. Some of the future drug barons, such as Pablo Escobar and Jose Santacruz, are believed to have started in the trade as mules. The few petty smugglers the U.S. authorities caught were merely deported to Colombia, where they were seldom prosecuted.

Heroin, not cocaine, was the main illegal drug on the DEA's radar screen in the mid 1970s. Yet, times were changing. For much of the twentieth century, cocaine had been mainly the drug of the elite and the jazz and Hollywood scenes, and because of its high cost, it became known as "the champagne of drugs." The so-called psychedelic revolution of the 1970s revived interest in drugs of all kinds and people began to view cocaine as a relatively safe high. Meanwhile, the DEA's lack of interest reflected the attitude of the U.S. government at all levels toward cocaine. In September, 1975, for example, a drug task force established by President Gerald Ford issued an report, concluding that "cocaine was not physically addictive and usually has not resulted in serious social consequences, such as crime or hospital emergency admissions, or both." The Task Force recommended that U.S. law enforcement focus on drugs, such as heroin, amphetamines and mixed barbiturates, which, it believed, posed more risk.

Official U.S. statistics painted a different picture. By 1974, 5.4 million Americans had acknowledged that they had tried using cocaine at least once. While law enforcement continued to focus on heroin in the late 1970s, the statistics documenting cocaine use shot up. By 1979, according to one estimate, at least 20 percent of Americans had used cocaine in the past year and 7.3 percent had used it during the previous month.

When President Jimmy Carter took the office in 1976, his administration also did not view cocaine use and abuse seriously. "Cocaine . . . is the most benign of illicit drugs currently in widespread use," wrote Dr. Peter Bourne, drug advisor to President Carter and his special assistant for health issues. "Short acting, not physically addicting and acutely pleasurable, cocaine has found increasing favor at all socioeconomic levels." The government's benign attitude set the tone.

"When the public heard government officials like Bourne downplay cocaine, they thought, 'Hey, cocaine is a recreational drug. I have nothing to worry about,'" said Michael Kuhlman, a retired DEA agent who joined the agency in 1970.

When Uncle Sam failed to see a major social trend unfolding in America, Colombia quickly became the linchpin of the Latin American drug trade and cocaine replaced heroin as the drug of choice in America. Colombian criminals, based primarily in Medellin and Cali quickly began to transform themselves from nondescript smugglers to the makings of drug kingpins. By the late 1970s, the drug trade boomed, and cocaine, with high profit margins, started to eclipse marijuana as the Colombian smuggler's preferred product.

The huge profits to be made from cocaine spurred the growth of highly organized, dynamic networks of traffickers. They had once used mules to smuggle their product to market, but now, to meet the increasing demand, they began using more sophisticated means, including private airplanes that ranged from old DC-3s to Cessna 210s to ultramodern Lear jets, as well as ships from the Colombian merchant marine fleet.

U.S. and Colombian law enforcement reported that smuggling routes were expanding to include not only flights directly from Bogota to Miami but also indirect routes involving Cali, Medellin, Barranquilla, and Buenaventura to places in Canada, Mexico, the Caribbean Islands, Central America and even Europe.

By 1980, two distinct trafficking groups centered in Cali and Medellin emerged as the major players in the country's drug trade. But of the two, the Medellin cartel was initially the most powerful. The cartel was named after the city of Medellin (population 1.5 million), the capital of Antioquia province. Historically, Medellin had a reputation as a smuggling center for liquor and cigarettes from the United States, and stereos, radio and televisions set form the ports of the Panama.

Medellin began playing an important role in the international drug trade in 1973, when Chilean General Augusto Pinochet overthrew President Salvador Allende and either jailed or deported numerous drug traffickers who had made Chile the center of the emerging cocaine trade. The trade then moved to Colombia, where several factors help explain the country's rise to dominance in the Latin American drug trade.

For one thing the coca plant is easy to grow, even in remote rugged terrain, which comprises a large part of the Colombian topography. The plant has a lifespan of about thirty years and can be harvested up to six times annually, which provides for an endless supply of raw material that makes up for drug seizures by law enforcement.

Moreover, geographically, Colombia is well situated to serve as the linchpin that receives coca leaves from Peru and Bolivia, process them into cocaine, and then transports the finished product by land and sea to the United States. Colombia is also a large country with vast forests and an area that can hide secretive air strips and laboratories and protect their illegal operation against effective attack by the Colombian military and law enforcement agencies.

The size of some of the drug–producing labs were remarkable. In one 1984 raid, code-named Operation Condor, authorities discovered six cocaine labs including a super lab in the process of being installed. It had pumps, steel vats, a 300-horspower generator and centrifuges capable of producing up to 60 pounds of cocaine a day. The complex even had a house for pilots, who, as they flew in to pick up the next cocaine shipment for the United States, would see a large inviting sign bearing the words, "*Welcome to Tranquilandia.*"

Other factors that help explain Colombia's rise to prominence in the illegal drug industry include the country's experience in exporting contraband, the lack of a significant government presence in many rural areas of the country, and a strong entrepreneurial tradition that it could apply to marketing and distribution of illegal drugs. In addition, the pervasive corruption in Colombian society, the growth of a large underground economy in the 1970s, a large Colombian population in the United States, segments of which provided cover for drug-trafficking activities and the use of a sophisticated distribution network once the drugs arrive in the United States, and the ruthless nature of the Colombian drug cartels especially the Medellin cartel.

"I have heard about the mafia in the U.S., but compared to ours they can be described as gentlemen when they kill," Juan Ferro, a journalist with *El Espectador,* a Colombian newspaper, explained to the author in the late 1980s. "The U.S. Mafia might send a note of apology to the next of kin. A capo (a Colombian drug trafficker boss) will kill you, your wife, your children, your relatives, f he can find them, and even your pets."

The leaders of the Medellin cartel – Pablo Escobar, Carlos Lehder, the Ochoa brothers (Jorge, Fabio and Juan David) and Jose Gonzalo Rodriguez Gacha –became known as *"Los Hampones"* (the Hoodlums) because of their backgrounds and rough criminal style. They came from the lower and blue-collar classes and clawed their way up the road to riches, using intimidation and violence.

Carlos Lehder was born in the Colombian coffee-growing region of Armenia, but his parents brought him to the U.S. at an early age. By age 15, he was dealing in cocaine.

Three years later he was arrested and convicted of import-
ing 200 pounds of marijuana into the United State. Lehder
served a two year prison term and was deported to Colombia in 1976, where he returned to the drug-trafficking business, learned to fly and organized a distribution ring that
specialized in aerial drug drops and eventually evolved into
the Medellin Cartel.

In a 1983 interview with the Colombian magazine *La
Semana,* Lehder described the Medellin cartel's early be-
ginnings. He had a predilection for flying, Lehder recalled,
and with the money he managed to bring with him after being kicked out of the United States, he went to the
Bahamas and bought his first airplane. By buying, repair-
ing and selling old planes, Lehder boasted of making his
first million dollars by age twenty-three. For $4.5 million
he bought Norman's Cay, a small island in the Bahamas,
where he built a radar-equipped airstrip that he used to
smuggle drugs into the U.S. via the short final hop to the
Florida coast.

Lehder's operational base became his home town of Armenia, where he founded a political movement, the National
Latin Movement, built a five-star hotel with a landmark
statue of The Beatles, John Lennon, a condominium complex with total area of 80, 000 square meters and established
a newspaper, *Quindio Libre,* which published techniques on
how to increase marijuana production. The U.S. government
filed an indictment against Lehder in Tampa, Florida in the

early 1980s, but when the Bahamas government raided Norman's Cay, he was gone. Lehder returned to Colombia but his importance in the Medellin Cartel diminished.

By 1987, the DEA and the Colombian government had put Lehder's net wealth at more than $3 billion. Lehder was one of the most eccentric drug kingpins of all time. Lehder got the nickname "Crazy Charlie" because of his bizarre and often unpredictable behavior. He had no qualms about using his mother as a drug courier or killing a young man at a party in Colombia who had spurned his homosexual advances. He memorized Hitler's *Mein Kampf* and would expound for hours on the "virtues" of the Nazi leader.

Indeed, he was a great admirer of both Nazi-icon Adolph Hitler and Marxist Che Guevara. Lehder hated the U.S. and viewed cocaine as a kind of atomic bomb that could destroy Uncle Sam from within. He also aspired to someday becoming president of Colombia and he used his illicit fortune to finance his political ambitions.

Jorge Luis Ochoa Vasquez, was another founding member of the Medellin cartel who has been portrayed by the Colombian actor, Joavanny Alvarez, in the TV series "*Escobar, El Patrón del Mal*" as the character of Pedro Motoa. Ochoa was responsible for transforming his family's business into a modern drug-trafficking organization. Born in Cali, Colombia, and raised in Evigado, Jorge Luis was the second of three sons of Fabio Ochoa Restrepo and Margot Vasquez.

The U.S. Drug Enforcement Administration first discovered Ochoa's role in drug trafficking in 1977 when they confiscated sixty pounds of cocaine in Miami. Ochoa had ostensibly gone to Miami as a manager of an import-export firm. But, in reality, he was a cocaine distributor for his uncle, Fabio. Although indicted, Ochoa escaped to Medellin, Colombia, where together with his father, Fabio, and brothers Fabio Jr. and Juan David, he continued to operate the family's cocaine-smuggling business.

In the early 1980s, the DEA office in Bogota reported that Ochoa "had become one of the most powerful traffickers in Medellin and the northern coast of Columbia, and is continuing to introduce one hundred to two hundred kilos of cocaine into the U.S. by several unknown methods."

Jorge Luis' two brothers also played important roles in the Medellin Cartel. In 1986, Jorge and his two brothers, were charged with several crimes including conspiracy to smuggle sixty tons of cocaine into the U.S. Fabio Jr., the youngest brother, lived for a time in Miami during the late 1970s, where he headed the family's drug distribution network. In the early 1980s he was implicated in the murders of drug informant Barry Seale.

But among the founding members of the Medellin cartel, none became more notorious and world famous than Pablo Escobar, El Patron. Born the son of a night watchman and a school teacher on December 1st in 1949, Escobar grew up in the tough blue-collar suburb of Envigado, a place that would later become his refuge when the Colombian authorities were in hot pursuit of him.

In a shrewd effort to create positive public image, Escobar often portrayed himself as coming from a poor, deprived background while in reality, his life was middle class (by Colombian standards), and he was a high school graduate, no small feat for someone from Envigado.

According to Pablo's brother, Roberto, Pablo knew what he wanted out of life from an early age: to be fabulously rich. As Roberto recalls, "Even as very young boy, he (Pablo) would tell his mother: 'Wait until I grow up, mom. I'm going to give you everything. Just wait until I grow up. Then later as he grew up, according to Roberto, Pablo vowed, "When I'm twenty-two years old, I want a million dollars. If I don't (get it), I'm going to kill myself. I'm going to put a bullet in my head."

In 1974, according to Roberto Escobar, Pablo studied political science at the University of Antiochia, with the ambition of becoming a criminal lawyer and eventually entering politics. Pablo's ultimate goal: the presidency of Colombia. But Pablo did not have the money to continue his studies and dropped out. According to other reports, however, Pablo told his mother that he was not cut out for school and that he had bigger plans in life. In 1982, Escobar did get elected to the Colombian Congress as an alternative representative.

Escobar's first known criminal activity has often been

described as stealing gravestones from cemeteries. According to the story, Pablo would sell gravestones to recently bereaved relatives of the deceased. Family members and writers who have studied Escobar's life have cast doubt on the truth of the story. Mark Bowden in his book, *Killing Pablo*, points out that Escobar was deeply superstitious. Bowden writes, "He (Escobar) subscribed to that peculiarly pagan brand of Catholicism common in rural Antioquia, one that prays to idols…and commutes with dead spirits. Stealing headstones would be an unlikely vocation for anyone who feared the spirit world."

According to Bowden's research, Escobar was a heavy life-time user of marijuana. Escobar would sleep "until one or two in the afternoon, lighting up not long after waking up, and staying stoned for the rest of the day or night."

By the time he was twenty, Escobar was a successful car thief who would pull drivers from their cars in broad day light and then strip the cars of their valuable part within hours. In the early 1970s, Escobar worked as a thief and bodyguard and made a quick $100,000 on the side kidnapping and ransoming a Medellin business executive. In 1976 police arrested Escobar for possessing 30 pounds of cocaine, but he never went to trial. Later, the drug trafficker had gunmen murdered the two arresting officers in what the beginning of a vicious pattern that he would follow throughout his criminal career: kill anyone who crossed him, stood in his way, or posed a threat.

In March 1976, Escobar, now twenty-six years old, married Maria Victoria who was 15 years old. Together they had two children, Juan Pablo and Manuela. The Escobars lived in a luxurious estate called Hacienda Nápoles (Spanish for Naples Estate) that Escobar designed. The estate covers about 7.7 square miles of land. It included a Spanish colonial house and a large zoo that included many kinds of animals from different continents such as giraffes, ostriches, elephants, antelope, and exotic birds. The ranch also had a large collection of old and luxurious cars and motorcycles, a private airport and even a cart racing track. Escobar planned to construct a Greek-style citadel near Hacienda Napoles, and although construction began, it was never finished.

From an early age, Escobar showed he had the ruthlessness to be a big crime boss. He would hire thugs to kidnap people who owed him money. He would seek a ransom from the kidnapped victim's family and if they refused to pay, he would kill them. Even if the ransom was paid, Escobar would kill his victims. The kidnapping of Diego Echavarria, a factory owner from Envigado, in the summer of 1971 was a case in point. Echavarria was strangled even though his family had paid a $50,000. Echavarria was highly unpopular among the poor in the area, and although it was never proven that Escobar had orchestrated the crime, it made him a local folk hero. According to Bowden, "The killing had all the hallmarks of the young crime boss's emerging style: cruel deadly, smart, and with an eye towards public relations."

Escobar shrewdly began cultivating a romantic image of a Robin Hood who stole from the establishment and gave to the poor. He developed "Medellin without Slums," a housing project for 1,000 poor families. Soccer was Pablo's passion, so he paid for lights that allowed children to play in the soccer fields at night. In respect for the gangster-benefactor, Colombians from all walks of life started to defer to him as Don Pablo. Escobar reveled in the legend he was becoming. Asked by a group of journalists, "Are you violent and arrogant?" Escobar replied, "Those who know me know I have good sense of humor and that I keep a smile on my face. And I'll say one thing: I always sing in the shower."

Those who saw Escobar in the flesh were startled to see how unremarkable he looked. Pudgy, soft-spoken and badly in need of a tailor. Escobar's ten-dollar haircut gave him the look of a greaser. His most distinctive feature was a black bristled mustache worn in the manner of his hero Pancho Villa, the Mexican outlaw and hero of the 1919-20 Mexican Revolution. Escobar was polite and formal in the company he kept and in the numerous letters he wrote to Colombian authorities over the years, sternly warning them to get off his back or face unspecified consequences.

Escobar relished his fame by always looked painfully uncomfortable in the glare or a television camera. To friend and foe alike, though, Escobar was man to be feared, and even respected, according to which side of the law one was on. In reality, he was a quick learner and natural leader, with an enterprising mind for business and an unforgiving memory.

"It's his eyes," one DEA agent explained. "He looks totally nondescript, but his eyes reveal the soul of a cunning cold-blooded killer."

By 1979, the year he turned 30, Escobar was helping to pioneer the use of aircraft to move illegal drugs. Six years later, he had clawed his way to top rung in the leadership of the Medellin cartel. A decade later, Forbes magazine named Escobar one of the world's richest men, calculating his personal fortune at $2.5 billion, or perhaps more, thanks to roughly the 80 percent share of the cocaine trade the DEA believed the Patron and his associates controlled. "Escobar was to cocaine what Ford was to automobiles," explained Thomas V. Cash, a retired DEA special agent who, in the 1990s, was in charge of the DEA's Miami office.

CHAPTER TWO

# THE GENTLEMAN FROM CALI

**T**HE MOST SERIOUS rival to Pablo Escobar and the Medellin cartel was the cartel from Cali, a city known for it music, fair weather and beautiful women. What became the Cali cartel, the most powerful drug trafficking mafia in history, has its origins in the late 1960s. The cartel's early history and the biographies of its principal founders – Gilberto and Miguel Rodriguez and Jose Santacruz – are shrouded in mystery, and accounts of their childhoods and family backgrounds conflict and are filled with contradictory details. Some published accounts have the founders coming from middle-class, professionally oriented families. Others say they come from more humble backgrounds. Indeed, finding reliable information about the cartel and its leaders became one of the major challenges facing law enforcement during the next three decades.

Santacruz and the Rodriguez brothers were masters

of fake identities, especially in the early years, when they carried bogus passports and other fake Colombian documents and traveled under many assumed names as a ploy to confuse investigators. The subterfuge was part of the Cali cartel's brilliant strategy to keep a low profile, portraying themselves as gentlemen and their organization as a gentler, more professional alternative to their violent rival 200 miles to the north in Medellin, led by Pablo Escobar.

In the years ahead, the Cali men would challenge, intimidate– even kill – anyone who attempted to expose this myth. Gilberto Rodriguez, for instance would often get on the phone and leave messages for reporters, chastising them for vsuggesting that he was involved in the drug trade. Colombian journalist, Maria Jimena Duzan, in her memoir *Death Beat* recalled how Rodriguez once called the newsroom at her newspaper, *El Espectador*, about the publication of an article that described a police raid on his daughter's house. Nothing had been found in the raid, and the police did not charge his daughter with a crime, Rodriguez pointed out. Then he added, "By the way, this violence is really terrible. You and I are both victims of Pablo Escobar. I understand what you are going through because I am in the same situation."

As late as the early 1990s, when the Cali cartel was acknowledged as the leading drug-trafficking mafia in the world, Rodriguez would still coyly play his innocence game with the press. In a rare – indeed extraordinary – interview with *Time* magazine in 1991, the drug lord *par excellence* claimed to be an honest businessman. His only crime, he said, was too much success. He had incurred official displeasure, Rodriguez told *Time*'s reporters, when he was chairman of the board of a bank in Cali and president of the board of directors of a bank in Panama that laundered money. Yes, he owned a Chrysler distributorship in Colombia but, the godfather joked, in a play on the name of Chrysler's boss, "Maybe people confuse coca with my dealings with [Lee] Iaccoca."

What is certain is that the Rodriguez brothers were natives of Mariquita in the department of Tolima and grew up in the poor Balthazar barrio of Cali. Gilberto was born in 1939 and Miguel in 1943. Gilberto apparently never finished highschool. In the 1991 *Time* article, Gilberto provided these details about his background, "I was born between the towns of Mariquita and Honda Tolima. My father was a painter and a draftsman, and my mother was a housewife. We were three brothers [the third was Jorge] and three sisters. When I was fifteen, I started work as a clerk in a drugstore in Cali. By the time I was twenty, I was the manager, and at twenty-five, ten years after entering the business, I quit in order to start my own drugstore."

Rodriguez added that he had seven children, six of whom were professionals and one who was a student. "They all got their degrees at US or European universities; most are now working in our businesses," Rodriguez revealed. In an article in July 1990, *Forbes* magazine reported that Miguel Rodriguez graduated from Colombia's San Buenaventura University, but Colombian investigative journalist, Fabio Castillo, uncovered proof that Miguel bought that degree.

In 1997, Guillermo Pallomari, a Cali Cartel accountant who became an informer for the U.S. government, testified that Miguel Rodriguez had bought a law degree with honors from the University de Santiago de Chile, and in return had donated a library to the university. Rodriguez had also bought personal items for Gonzalo Paz, the dean of the university.

One newspaper reported that Gilberto began working for a drugstore at age thirteen, delivering legal drugs to customers. Younger brother Miguel also worked in a drugstore as a youngster. A decade later, Gilberto would become famous in Colombia as the owner of a chain of drugstores known as *Drogas La Rebaja*. The Rodriguez brothers reportedly began their life of crime as teenagers, and quite early in life they exhibited the leadership qualities that would carry them to the top of the criminal world; not least, it seems, a propensity for violence. According to Castillo, "They commanded the respect of like gangs because they were highly dangerous individuals."

Castillo reported how Gilberto and brother Miguel were arrested for counterfeiting money, but the female judge who was to try the case received death threats and let the statute of limitations on the trial run out. The background details of Jose Santacruz Londono are spotty as well. According to one confidential DEA informant, Santacruz, who was born in 1943, went to high school with the Rodriguezes and became boyhood friends with them.

On 30 October 1969, the Bogota-based newspaper *El Espectador* published a biography of Santacruz in which his wife told the reporter that he was the father of one girl and had recently completed four years of engineering at De Valle University of the Andes in Bogota. They lived in Bogota in an apartment building in the Quinta Paredes district, she claimed. The article revealed that Santacruz had been implicated in the kidnappings of a university student and an industrialist in Bogota and had recently bought three taxis in Bogota for 192,000 pesos in cash. The newspaper made no connection between the kidnappings and the fleet of taxis, but readers must have wondered how an engineering student could afford a taxi fleet.

The three men who would found the Cali cartel were involved in the kidnapping of a fisherman when they were teenagers, according to one source who knew them during the time, but managed to avoid conviction, although Gilberto did spend one day in jail. By 1969 they had become part of a kidnapping organization know as *Las Chemas*, run by a veteran criminal called Luis Fernando Tamayo Garcia. The gang was implicated in the successful kidnapping of two Swiss citizens: diplomat Herman Buff and student Werner Jose Straessle.

In June 1995, an article in *El Tiempo* newspaper reported that Gilberto was twenty-eight at the time of the kidnapping, and leader of the seven gang members involved in the crime. The three Cali cartel founders reportedly used the twelve million pesos (about $700,000) they were paid for their hostages as seed money to bankroll their entry into the world of drug trafficking.

Law enforcement officials who were familiar with the mob's history say it is remarkable that for more than thirty years the Rodriguez brothers and Santacruz were able to remain close friends and allies and maintain a relationship not normally found in the cutthroat world of crime. "In all my years of studying the Cali cartel, I never knew the Rodriguez brothers or Santacruz to have any serious disagreement," said Sandy Hill, a DEA intelligence analyst. "They all seemed to know their role and were focused on making money."

Ed Kacerosky, a customs agent who worked on the watershed Operation Cornerstone investigation in the early 1990s (see Chapter 10), agrees that money was the motivation for their close relationship, but added that the cartel's board of directors banded close together for another important reason: survival. "They realized they had to stick together because the Medellin cartel was out to destroy them," Kacerosky said. When Helmer "Pacho" Herrera became one of the cartel's key players, Santacruz and the Rodriguez brothers seemed to accept Pacho's homosexuality.

THE GENTLEMAN FROM CALI

"It was very strange," recalled one DEA agent. "From the accounts I heard, they tolerated Pacho. They would giggle among themselves about his homosexual behavior, but Pacho would go off and do his thing and business was business."

Interestingly, reports suggest that all three founders had guerrilla sympathies, at least early in their life. One source told the British journalist, Simon Strong, that the three were "friends of the founders of the *ELN* (National Liberation Army), so much so that they took part in the 1969 kidnapping of the two Swiss men to finance the *ELN*."The *ELN* was one of several armed Marxist groups dedicated to the overthrow of the Government, others included *FARC* (the Revolutionary Armed Forces of Colombia) and M-19.

Each of the Cali cartel founders had his own style, which helped them to build their criminal organization. Gilberto; short, goateed and overweight, looked innocuous enough, but he became known as the "Chess Player" for his ruthless and calculating approach to the drug business. In the beginning, the Chess Player would be a hands-on manager, but he eventually stepped back and became responsible for the organization's strategic planning. The handsome but cold eyed Miguel, his younger brother, was a micromanager who liked to be involved in the smallest details of the cartel's day to- day operations and was, by all accounts, a difficult boss to work for. "The people who worked for the Cali cartel looked on Gilberto as being like a kindly uncle," recalled Ruben Prieto, a DEA agent who investigated the mob. "They liked him. On the other hand they were scared to death of Miguel."

Jose Santacruz was stocky, rugged-looking and low key. Known as "Chepe" to his associates and pursuers, he was the most violent of three founders. He was also known as "*El Gordo*" – the fat man – for his love of food. Chepe became invaluable as coordinator of the cartel's international co-caine transportation network. The DEA published a "most wanted" photo of him in the early 1980s, when he was a fugitive. He wore a beard and looked like a dead ringer for Franco Harris, the great Pittsburgh Steelers running back of the 1970s.

Pacho Herrera, who would rise to become number four in the hierarchy, returned to Cali from the U.S. in 1983 af-ter a getting started in short prison term and negotiated an arrangement with the cartel founders over supply and dis-tribution rights, which allowed him to build a base in New York City. Herrera was later made a member of the cartel's board of directors, and proved invaluable to the mafia by using his contacts to help open up Mexico for their pow-ders. The Chess Player, Miguel and Chepe moved into the drug trade as opportunities opened up in the early 1970s.

The leading Colombian trafficker of this period was Benjamin Herrera Zuleta, known as the "Black Pope of Cocaine," who had set up a cocaine distribution network based in Cali. In June 1975, he was captured smuggling a huge shipment. Released in March 1976, the Black Pope settled quietly in the Antioquia Department in central Colombia, but by then he had pioneered trafficking routes into the United States that the young, ambitious traffickers of Cali would use.

The cartel founders at first dabbled in marijuana smuggling, but soon saw the huge profits to be made from cocaine. Marijuana, after all, involved a lot of risk, since one had to ship large volumes of the product to earn big profits. On the other hand, cocaine could be bought for $15,000 a kilo in Colombia and sold on the streets of the United States for as much as $50,000 a kilo in the mid-1970s. Moreover, you did not need big ships or planes to do it.

Using the seed money they had made from kidnapping, together with some of their drug profits, the Cali founders bought a small light plane, which they used to ship larger amounts of coca back to the Valle del Cauca, the province of which Cali is capital city. But with little experience in the trade, they quickly ran afoul of the law. In November 1975, Gilberto was captured in Peru with 180 kilos of coca paste aboard a light plane. Released a short time later, he was arrested again in 1977, this time in New York, where he had come to look over the market.

The other partners also had their run-ins with the law as they worked to build their criminal empire. Records indicate that Santacruz was arrested twice during the 1970s, the first time in 1976 while traveling from New York City to

Costa Rica and the second in 1977 on a weapons charge in Queens, New York. Pacho Herrera, who started his criminal career smuggling relatively small amounts of cocaine into New York City, was arrested in 1975 and 1979, according to DEA reports.

On 10 September 1975, the Colombian Customs Agency filed this brief report on the state of drug trafficking in Colombia:

Valle del Cauca:

58 – Rodriguez Orejuela, Gilberto, drug trafficker.

Address: No. 44E-27 4th Avenue, Cali.

62 – Rodriguez Orejuela, Miguel, drug trafficker.

Gilberto and Miguel were fifty-eighth and sixty-second on a list of the 113 top drug traffickers in the country. They were certainly moving up in the criminal world. Gilberto emerged as the gang's early leader, and according to Castillo's investigation, sent his boyhood friend, Hernando Giraldo Soto, to the United States to make contact. Giraldo Soto ran the organization's operation out of New York City for three years, and during the period from March through October 1978 made at least $2.6 million in drug deals. When law enforcement busted the point man, Gilberto replaced him with another close associate, Jose Santacruz.

As the 1970s progressed, the Cali cartel strengthened and refined its network, became better organized, and began using its family and criminal contacts and the Colombian émigré community in the United States to further its criminal enterprise. The emerging Cali cartel went quietly about its business creating a market for cocaine in New York City.

At the time the city was known as the heroin capital of the United States, and the Cali men had a big jump on law enforcement, whose attention was elsewhere.

The aspiring drug kingpins turned the city of Cali into a company town. In Cali, the cartel controlled the public telephone lines and was able to tap in to them virtually at will. Meanwhile, the Rodriguez brothers paid as many as 5,000 taxi drivers to be their eyes and ears in the city. "As soon as you landed in Cali, [the brothers Rodriguez] knew who you were," said Chris Feistl, a DEA agent who investigated the Cali cartel in the 1990s. "It was impossible to do anything in Cali without the cartel knowing about it."

That was the frustration in investigating the gangsters in Cali, which the DEA was learning fast. The phone company was not the only local institution that their money and power had compromised. In the early 1980s, the cartel began turning Cali into a company town. The Rodriguez brothers and Santacruz controlled Cali in the way that feudal barons once ruled medieval estates. Miguel and Gilberto Rodriguez's base was the center of Cali (Normandia, Juanabu, Los Cristales) and the center of the downtown area around the Intercontinental Hotel, as well as a large portion of the upscale Ciudad Jardin area. Santacruz controlled the southern area of Cali (Ingenio 1 and Ingenio 2), and Pacho Herrera controlled a city south of Cali, Jamundi, and the areas around Yumbo and Palmira north of Cali.

Inside their enclaves, the godfathers built palatial estates that flaunted their success as "businessmen." In 1989, *Money* magazine described Miguel Rodriguez's four-bedroom home (not including servant's quarters) as having "it all." The magazine provided details: "Seven living rooms, each in a different style, are packed with expensive furniture, a real stuffed lion and lion-skin rug, plus hundreds of Lladro porcelain figurines that cost $2,000 to $3,000 each. A curtain of clear glass beads hangs from the ceiling on the second floor down to an indoor reflecting pool. Spiral staircases at either end of the house lead down on one side to a Jack Lalanne size sky lit gym and [on] the other side to a bar with an underwater view of the outdoor pool."

The overlords had money and power, but they wanted status too. So they began working hard to have Cali's movers and shakers accept them. Chepe, for instance, liked to throw lavish parties for government officials, providing food, drink and entertainment for 6-700 people at a time. But it was not easy at first. Club Colombia, an exclusive social club for businessmen and industrialists, rejected Chepe's application for membership. The enraged drug lord did not go out and murder the snobs. Instead, he built an exact replica of the club on a hillside in the upscale subdivision of Ciudad Jardin and named it Casa Noventa. Chepe also built his own country club outside the city, Villa

Brenda, complete with a bridge, statutes of Cali's heroes, and three large white religious crosses.

The Rodriguez brothers used their cocaine profits to build a business empire that penetrated every section of Cali's economic life. Their organization employed about twenty tax accountants, economists and financial consultants, who worked exclusively on its business and money-laundering activities. In 1974, the Banco de Trabajadores was founded with a $500,000 grant from two foundations that were created to strengthen and organize labor in Latin America.

Gilberto Rodriguez managed to gain control of the bank and was appointed chairman of the board of directors. He then gave shares of stocks to local leaders as a token of friendship, appointed some of them to the board of directors, and granted loans and allowed overdrafts on their checking accounts.

The brothers chose to adopt a business-like approach to building their drug trafficking empire. They treated cartel members like company employees, hiring the best people for the job after they had filled out an application and had an interview. Successful applicants were faxed a list of rules, a company contract so to speak. "Live modestly" and "avoid attracting attention to yourself" were two of the major rules. Even people who operated stash houses were expected to leave the house in the morning and return at night like a typical working class person.

The brothers had developed their own style in running

the business. Gilberto became known as the Chess Player for his ruthless and calculating approach to the drug business. Although he began as a hands-on manager, he eventually stepped back to take charge of the cartel's strategic planning. Miguel, on the other hand, was known as an intense micromanager. "Miguel used the phone and fax to run the cartel from Cali," said Harold Ackerman, who ran the Cali's Miami base in the early 1990s, and eventually testified against the brothers, "He was constantly on the phone with me, wanting to know every little detail."

Cartel looked upon Gilberto as being like a kindly uncle—they liked him," explained retired DEA agent Ruben Prieto. "On the other hand, they were scared to death of Miguel."

The Rodriguez brothers went about building its criminal empire quietly, downplaying violence and terror as the principle means of achieving its objective. In reality, of course, the Cali cartel was not the kinder, gentler mafia that their propaganda machine brilliantly portrayed them to be.

The Cali Cartel could be as vicious as the next group of gangsters when it needed to be.

Miguel Rodriguez, for instance, had no qualms about killing the husband (a fellow drug trafficker) of a woman he desired. Claudio Endo, an associate of Miguel Rodriguez, had killed a couple of guerrillas, one of whom owed him money. Unfortunately for Endo, one of the guerrillas was a friend of Pacho Herrera.

Pacho received permission from the other three cartel godfathers (the Rodriguez brothers and Santacruz) to kill Endo. About 2 A.M. on an early March day in 1994, Endo was sleeping at his ranch near Jamundi when a couple of carloads of gunmen arrived, on orders of the Cali cartel. They surprised Endo and proceeded to torture him and mutilate his body with submachine gunfire. Claudia Endo was there but was taken away unharmed. Six to eight months later, Miguel Rodriguez and Claudia were lovers.

A confidential informant told DEA agents that Chepe had Fuquen killed because she was planning to leave Colombia for Miami with his kids. The drug lord thought she was planning to take them away from him and he would never see them again. "The CI told us that Marely was always yelling and screaming and complaining, and Chepe was not the type of guy who would put up with that forever," said Robinson. It was just that the self-styled gentlemen from Cali usually did their violence without much noise.

Pacho Herrera would invite guests whom he believed had betrayed him to his sprawling hacienda, El Desierto, outside Cali. There he would feed them, take them into a room, put a bag over their head, torture them until they confessed, kill them, and then dump their bodies in the Cauca River at night, all neatly done without waking up the neighbors.

The gentlemen from Cali had another unique way of dealing with some of their suspected traitors and screwups. They would invite them to come to Cali by airplane, and then kill them. Rather than dump their bodies in the Cauca River, they would find somebody that looked like them, give the substitute the dead person's papers and plane ticket, and then send them back to where the dead person had come from. When the dearly departed was reported missing, the cartel could always say, "Hey, don't blame us. He took the plane and went back to where he came from."

It was years before the good guys discovered the cartel's presence. "They were big before we knew it," said Rich Crawford, a former DEA agent who investigated the cartel in the late 1970s and 1980s. "It took a long time before we were able to convince the higher ups [in the DEA] that a growing, sophisticated drug trafficking group from Cali, Colombia, was operating in our city right under our nose.

# CHAPTER THREE

# CO-EXISTENCE

**T**HE CALI AND the Medellin cartels had starkly contrast-
ing philosophies toward criminal enterprise, but initially, during the period from the late 1970s through
the early 1980s years, they were on basically good relations.
According to intelligence sources, Cali and Medellin collaborated on making joint shipments, setting up processing
labs, planning assassinations, coordinating their operations,
and working together to corrupt the political growing the
criminal enterprise process.

As Rennselaer Lee, author of *The White Labyrinth: Cocaine
and Political Power* and *The Andean Cocaine Industry* and an
expert on the drug trade, pointed out, "Cocaine barons share a
common political agenda that includes blocking the extradition of drug traffickers, the criminal justice system, and selec-
tively persecuting the Colombian left." Former DEA agent
Michael Kane, head of the DEA's Medellin office from 1981

to 1984, said that the Cali and Medellin cartels were friendly competitors through the mid-1980s. "They were not at each other's throats in those days," said Kane. "They had their own markets and there was enough room for both of them."

At this time, the leaders of the Cali and Medellin cartels mingled with each other, enjoying their growing wealth and moving freely in society. Both Pablo Escobar and the Rodriguez brothers, for instance, got involved in auto racing – Escobar and a partner owned a share of a Renault team and the Rodriguez brothers owned two racing circuits. Drug traffickers heavily patronizing motor racing and, always looking to make more money, attempted to smuggle cocaine to the United States inside racing cars involved in competitions. Colombian police, acting on a tip from the DEA, thwarted their plans and seized thirty kilos of cocaine.

A November 1981 meeting of the "who's who" of Colombian drug trafficking was the high point of this Cali-Medellin collaboration. On November 12th, the leftist guerrilla group of April 19 Movement, more commonly known as M-19, swooped in on the University of Antioquia, kidnapped Marta Nieves Ochoa, the sister of the Ochoa family, and held her for ransom. Earlier, leftist guerrillas had tried to kidnap Carlos Lehder, wounding him in the attempt. The traffickers were incensed. They also had no intention of paying the outrageous ransom of nearly $15 million that the guerrillas were reportedly demanding for Marta's release.

Historians disagree about where the watershed meeting was held (Cali or Medellin) and how many attended (the numbers range from twenty to 223), but it is certain that the drug traffickers adopted a strategy that would not only free Marta Ochoa but also deal with the guerrilla threat. Leaflets were dropped at a soccer field in Cali, announcing the birth of a new organization, *Meurte a Secuestradores* (Death to Kidnappers), or *MAS*, as it became commonly known, and warning that their common defense group would see to it that those responsible for the kidnapping were "hung from all the trees in public parks or shot and marked with the sign of our group – MAS."

According to Pablo's brother Roberto, Pablo told one reporter, "If there was not an immediate and strong response, the M-19 were going to continue screwing our own families. We paid law enforcement 80 million pesos for the information they had at this moment and the next day they (the guerrillas) began to fall. My soldiers took them to our secret houses, our secret ranches, and people from law enforcement were there and we hung them and began to beat them up." The hapless guerillas were brutalized and many had their limbs cut off. Several guerrilla leaders were killed. For instance, the M-19's Antioquia leader was found stripped and buried in a Bogota car park.

The guerrillas got the message and released Marta unharmed, although it's unclear whether any ransom was paid. According to Guy Guglliotta and Jeff Leen, authors of *Kings of Cocaine*, the talks (regarding the Marta Nieves kidnapping) took place in Panama over several weeks, most likely under the auspices of the Panamanian armed forces, and with the participation of at least one Panamian government. None other than Panama's General Manuel Noriega, at the time the country's chief of military intelligence, was believed to have supervised the negotiations. After the communique was written, the meeting adjourned and everybody was present, which included members of the Cali and Medellin cartels, invited to a big finca or ranch outside Medellin. There, the drug kingpins ate, drank, chatted and enjoyed each other's company.

At another meeting of *MAS*, the drug lords reached agreement about how coke shipments would be regulated and coordinated to increase their profits and what group would control which market. The Cali cartel would have New York, the Medellin cartel would have Miami and South Florida. California was left up for grabs. According to journalist Fabio Castillo, the California market eventually ended up in the hands of Cali. The Ochoas and Escobar dominated the two meetings of *MAS*, and it appears at this point the Cali men was willing to defer to the Medellin leadership.

The relationship between Jorge Ochoa and Gilberto Rodriguez in the early 1980s illustrated well the groups' coexistence. Jorge Ochoa grew up in Cali, where he became a boyhood friend of Gilberto. In the late 1970s, the two became business partners and founded their own bank, the First InterAmericas Bank, as a way of laundering their money. According to Castillo, "The drug traffickers are said to have made a tacit pledge to the Panamanian government not to collect interest on deposits that they made in Panamanian banks. The earnings of these banks are simply handed over to the local government."

In the early 1980s, the more high profile Medellin cartel instead of the low key Cali cartel, became the main focus of U.S. law enforcement efforts. Alexander F. Watson, the deputy chief of missions at the U.S. Embassy in Bogota from 1981 to 1984, said that the mission viewed Cali as a relatively quiet city during that period. "The drug trade was just starting to explode," Watson recalled. "Back then, if you were an American, you could drive to Cali from Bogota any time you wanted without fear of danger."

The U.S. government maintained a benign view of the traffickers from Cali all through the 1980s. In explaining why the U.S. did not pay more attention to Cali, Cresencio Arcos, a career foreign service diplomat and the U.S. deputy assistant secretary for Latin America from 1987 to 1989 said, "Our sense was that the thugs from Medellin were more insidious. Escobar was your typical gold chain, fancy-car gangster who liked the flamboyant lifestyle. The traffickers from Cali, on the other hand, were low key and manipulative. We called them *criminals with Gucci slippers.*"

The DEA had opened branch offices in Cali and Medellin in 1981. Working as an agent in Colombia was not
without risk. In November 1976, Octavio Gonzalez, the
DEA chief in Bogota, was shot dead. The assassin, Thomas
Charles Coley, an American citizen, was able to walk into
Gonzalez's office at DEA headquarters on the top floor of
the Ugi Building without anyone checking his identity.

Coley killed Gonzalez with a .9 millimeter pistol. The
brazen assassination was a foreshadowing of the violence
that the Colombian drug trade would later generate. The
two DEA offices kept a low profile and neither had more
than two agents. The DEA received bits of intelligence
about the *MAS* meetings and began trying to gather information and cultivate sources and informants from the local
drug smuggling scene.

According to Michael Kuhlman, a DEA agent who
worked in the agency's Cali office in the early 1980s, "At
this time there were all kinds of traffickers in Colombia
who didn't work for the Medellin or Cali cartels. They were
small timers who trafficked in ten to twenty-kilo shipments
to the United States, as well as Canada and Europe."

The DEA's office in Cali also spent time trying to verify
the intelligence that Group Five in New York City had
gathered in their investigation of the Santacruz organization. "There was all kinds of misinformation about Chepe
Santacruz – his physical appearance, his false passports –
and one of our jobs was to sort it out," said Kuhlman. One

day, Kuhlman went to see the principal of a high school that Chepe's daughter had attended and graduated from eighth grade. The principal gave him a videotape of the graduation ceremony. It included some footage of Santacruz. Looking at the videotape, Kuhlman figured that he was about 5'8" tall and 180 pounds, very different vital stats than Kuhlman had seen in the reports.

A little while later, the agent learned that he did not have to go far to find Chepe. He had an office on the twelfth floor of the largest building in Cali, located about 100 yards from the DEA's office.

In 1983, the Colombian authorities began wiretapping Chepe's telephone calls to the United States. By October, the DEA verified that Santacruz had three Colombian bank accounts and his wife, Ampara, had an account at the Banco de Ponce in Miami. One of Santacruz's lawyers visited all the antinarcotics agencies in Colombia to warn them that he was planning to obtain an order from a local judge that would prohibit the police from intercepting any or all telephones belonging to Santacruz. By this time, the Cali cartel had on their payroll a team of talented lawyers handling their legal affairs. The Colombian authorities believed an employee in a telephone company had compromised their investigation by telling Santacruz about the government's wiretaps.

Then on 17 April 1984, the head of the Cali antinarcotics unit received a letter, written by Chepe Santacruz and addressed to the manager of the Cali telephone company. "I am aware that three telephone numbers in my name are being intercepted and I want to know if the intercepts have been authorized by a judge," Chepe demanded. The Colombian authorities believed that, once again, a telephone company employee on the cartel's payroll had once again compromised their investigation.

The authorities instructed the telephone company to discontinue the wiretaps, while they made plans to install wiretaps at points other than the central telephone switching station. As shown by the Colombian police's experience in trying to monitor Chepe's telephones, the godfathers were privy to anything happening in their city that impacted on their business interests or threatened their freedom.

During the 1980s, the Cali cartel developed a formidable security and intelligence network that corrupted the state and made it difficult for Colombian authorities to investigate. Their communications expertise was such that they were able to intercept police and military phone calls within the government and even to intercept phone calls made from the United States embassy. Carlos Espinosa (aka "Pinchalito") was the head of the cartel's communications. In his Miami courtroom testimony in 1997, Guillermo Pallomari, the cartel's chief accountant, noted that Espinosa had great influence at the telephone company in Cali, which allowed him to intercept about 400 calls a month.

In 1984, Gilberto Rodriguez and Jorge Ochoa journeyed together to Spain to escape the pressure that the Colombian government was exerting on the country's drug traffickers and to explore the European market for cocaine. The two friends and associates assumed aliases and posed as respectable business men, but they began enjoying an opulent lifestyle that attracted attention. Gilberto lived in a plush hotel and bought two Mercedes and two apartments, while Ochoa purchased four Mercedes and an 8,000-square-foot mansion with a discotheque, swimming pools and tennis courts. The Madrid authorities took notice of the wealthy visitors from South America and began investigating.

Discovering that warrants had been issued for their arrests in the United States, Spanish authorities began wiretapping their residence in September 1984. On October 17th, the police arrested Ochoa and Rodriguez. The U.S. Ambassador in Spain immediately requested their extradition to the United States.

Meanwhile, tension had developed between Pablo Escobar and the state of Colombia. During the Colombia's drug trade's formative period, the Cali and Medellin cartels operated in their home country with virtual impunity. However, by the mid-1980s the United States government was pressuring Colombia to abandon its laissez faire policy. President Ronald Reagan had declared the War on Drugs in 1982, and the U.S. shifted the focus of its interdiction efforts from heroin in Asia to cocaine in Latin America. Uncle Sam recognized Colombia as the hub of the region's drug trade.

Two years later, Rodrigo Lara Bonilla, Colombia's justice minister, reopened the case involving Pablo Escobar's arrest in 1976 on drug possession charges. Escobar was at the time serving as an alternate delegate to the Colombia Congress. He had higher political aspirations, but Don Pablo, as many now respectfully called the drug baron, suddenly found himself in the harsh and uncomfortable glare of public scrutiny.

Stripped away was the image of Don Pablo, leading citizen. Exposed was the reality – Pablo Escobar, drug lord. Escobar sued Lara for libel, sniffing, "I'm a victim of a persecution campaign," but eventually dropped out of public life, humiliated and fixated on revenge. Lara Bonilla received death threats, but ignored them. He was determined to investigate Escobar and go after the country's mafia.

In 1984, Lara authorized the spectacular raid on Tranquilandia, the major cocaine processing plant in the Amazon region. He paid for it with his life. A few months later, *sicarios* machine-gunned him to death on a residential street in Bogota. The justice minister's murder compelled president Belisario Bentacourt to declare a "war without quarter" against all drug traffickers, and the Medellin cartel godfathers did a disappearing act from public life.

The Cali godfathers did not approve of Lara Bonilla's assassination, but they were forced to go underground as well. That was the time when Gilberto Rodriguez and his friend Jorge Ochoa had left for Spain, and Santacruz traveled to Mexico and sent some his lieutenants to the United States to investigate possible locations for new cocaine processing labs.

At 11.40 A.M. on 6 November 1985, approximately thirty-five M-19 guerrillas stormed the Colombian Palace of Justice, located on Bogota's central Plaza de Bolivar. Within minutes, the guerrillas had 250 hostages, including Alfonso Reyes Echandia, the chief justice of Colombia's Supreme Court, and many of the twenty-four Supreme Court justices. For the next twenty-four hours, thousands of soldiers and police tried to retake the building, but the heavily armed and well entrenched guerrillas fought them off. When the government finally prevailed, twenty-five hostages lay dead, including Chief Justice Reyes, and apparently all the guerrillas.

It is widely believed the Medellin cartel paid the guerrillas to take the Palace and burn the extradition case files in the court archives, which contained incriminating evidence against them. The justices, many of whom favored upholding the extradition treaty with the United States, were scheduled to vote on the issue in the near future. The shocking attack on the heart of the Colombian legal system set the tenor for the rest of the decade. By 1990, more than

200 court officials and at least forty Colombian judges had been murdered.

Colombian President Virgilio Barco, who took office in 1986, implemented the Colombia–United States extradition treaty. The Medellin cartel responded by launching a ruthless terrorist campaign against the state. Calling themselves "*The Extraditables*," the cartel vowed, "Better a grave in Colombia than a jail in the United States" and began to target prominent supporters of extradition, as well as get-tough-on-drugs officials.

On 17 November 1986, *sicarios* murdered Colonel Jaime Ramirez Gomez, the head of the Anti-Narcotics Unit of the Colombian National Police. The following month, a killer on a motorcycle wove through the downtown Bogota traffic and shot Guillermo Cano to death. Guillermo Cano was the crusading antidrug editorial writer for *El Espectador*, Colombia's second largest newspaper.

In January 1988, near the Medellin airport in Rionegro, gunmen ambushed an automobile carrying Carlos Mauro Hoyos Jiminez. After killing Hoyos's bodyguard and chauffeur, the thugs dragged the bleeding attorney general out from his limousine, put him in a car, and sped away. President Barco ordered a manhunt, and authorities found Hoyos's body a few miles away from where security forces a few hours earlier had freed the kidnapped Andres Pastrana Arango, the Conservative party candidate for mayor (and future president of Colombia). Pastrana told the author in

1988 that Hoyos's killers had planned to kidnap Hoyos and others to dramatize their opposition to extradition.

Escobar and the Medellin cartel was at war with the state. The Cali cartel knew it was bad for business, but soon they would be at war with the Medellin cartel.

# CHAPTER FOUR

# COMING TO A HEAD

I N THE BEGINNING, the Cali and Medellin cartels engaged in peaceful co-existence. In 1981, they had participated in a meeting that organized *MAS* to deal with the guerrilla threat, and for the next three years, their members met in Colombian bars, discos, and haciendas to discuss business. When Gilberto Rodriguez and Jorge Ochoa left for Spain together, they trusted each other and worked together to explore new markets without fear of a double cross.

The U.S. market for cocaine was starting to become saturated by the mid-1980s. The street price had dropped nearly two-thirds, while cocaine was selling for four times as much in Europe. The Cali cartel saw that the European drug market was ripe for penetration. When Gilberto Rodriguez and Jorge Ochoa moved to Spain in 1984, they bought a large ranch in Badajoz, near the border with Portugal, to serve as a base of operations from which they could analyze the potential for trafficking cocaine in Europe.

The Cali cartel reached out to tobacco smugglers from Galicia in Spain, who had a good knowledge of the region's coastline and storage facilities that could be used to smuggle drugs.

The cartel began to use boats to pick up the drugs from ocean-going vessels and bring them ashore. To launder its money, it set up a network of accounts between Spanish and Panamanian banks and invested in real estate. Jorge Ochoa sent one of his key lieutenants, Teodoro Castrillon, to England, Germany and Holland to establish contacts with the local Colombian communities and to see if they could develop the infrastructure and distribution networks similar to those they had in the United States.

A potentially important market was the United Kingdom, which had seen an explosion in

heroin consumption from the late 1970s onwards but did not as yet have a significant coke problem. In 1985, a female cousin of the Ochoas opened up a supply line with her English husband Keith Goldsworthy, a pilot. Goldsworthy would fly hundreds of kilos into the U.S. in his private Cessna and then ship them to England. A parallel supply route was opened up by Fabio Ochoa, who personally met Goldsworthy on a visit to London. Within a year, cocaine seizures in the UK had doubled. Goldsworthy was eventually caught in Miami and jailed for twenty-two years, but by then the genie was out of the bottle.

Four years after the arrival of Rodriguez and Ochoa in Spain, the Cali cartel had made significant inroads in a drug market long dominated by heroin. "The major drug of choice in Europe in the late 1980s was heroin supplied by the Asians," said John Constanzo, a DEA agent who worked in Italy in the 1980s. "But the Cali cartel showed up on the DEA's radar screen, and we began seeing substantial increases in cocaine seizures." Surveys conducted in the countries of the European Community verified these observations. Cocaine seizures skyrocketed from 900 kilograms in 1985 to thirteen tons in 1990.

Two years later Miguel Solans, a government delegate for Spain's National Plan on Drugs, commented, "Although it is obvious that even if heroin is the drug that produces the most instability and deaths in Europe, the level of cocaine traffic and cocaine consumption has been rising at an alarming rate in recent years." Three years later, the cartel had so refined the European smuggling network that they were using many of the major commercial ports in Europe, including Hamburg, Liverpool, Genoa and Rotterdam.

As events in Europe showed, in the mid 1980s, the Cali and Medellin cartels realized that harmony in the drug trade was good for business. It was also good for Colombia. Pablo Escobar's brother, Roberto, explained how many thousands of Colombians were employed in the business form the workers in the jungle to the police. And many others benefited from the public works each of the traffickers did. According to Roberto, although Pablo eventually went to war with the Colombian state and with the Cali cartel, "At this time, there was very little violence within the business. Instead it was just making money, making more money…"

But relations went steadily downhill as the two powerful mafias expanded their operations and tension developed between them. Colombian and U.S. officials are unsure as to what caused the rift, but relations were not helped by the events following the extradition of Gilberto Rodriguez and Jorge Ochoa from Spain to Colombia in 1986. Gilberto and Jorge and their wives, however, were arrested near Rodriguez's apartment in Madrid. The United States sent a lawyer to Madrid to secure the extradition of Rodriguez and Ochoa, but the Spanish court extradited the two to Colombia instead.

Rodriguez went to trial in March 1987 on cocaine smuggling charges that could have led

to his extradition to the United States, but it took place in the company town where the Cali cartel owned everything, including the legal system.

Agent Rich Crawford, who was now stationed in the DEA's Tampa office, traveled to Colombia to testify. He had no illusions about the trial's outcome but was eager to testify as a way of showing that the DEA was not afraid to go into the cartel's home territory and rip off its phony cover of respectability.

Crawford arrived in Cali on March 17th and became the only DEA agent ever to testify at a trial in Colombia. His testimony was never allowed in court, however, and after three days, the judge acquitted Rodriguez. As a result, Rodriguez could not be extradited to the U.S. to be tried for the same offense, thanks to the double jeopardy clause of the U.S. Constitution.

When Jorge Ochoa returned to Colombia in July 1986, he faced a tougher legal situation than his friend Gilberto. He would first have to stand trial in Cartagena for smuggling 125 bulls into Colombia in 1981 and then face a drug charge in Medellin. If convicted, he could be extradited to the United States. Ochoa was found guilty and sentenced to two years in jail, but pending the appeal, the judge released Ochoa on $11,500 bond, conveniently overlooking the fact that he faced a more serious criminal charge in Medellin. The judge ordered Ochoa to report to the court every two weeks. The drug lord thanked the judge and opted to walk away.

Ochoa remained a fugitive until November 1986, when police stopped him at the toll gate near Palmira in the vicinity of Cali. He was on his way to the summit meeting called by Pablo Escobar to work out the details for creating a single, super cartel that Escobar would head. According to reports, Rafael Cardona, one of the Cali's contacts to the Medellin cartel, tipped off police that Ochoa would be driving a white Porsche in the Cali area. Cardona wanted to get even with Ochoa for having an affair with his girlfriend. When a police officer stopped Ochoa's car, Cardona's girlfriend was seated in the front seat. The drug lord casually offered the officer a $10 bribe but the officer refused. The bribe offer climbed to $400,000, but to no avail. Ochoa was arrested and put in a maximum security prison in Bogota. Meanwhile, the United States requested for his extradition.

The police had arrested Ochoa while the drug lord's surveillance helicopter circled above. Obviously, the threat of arrest did not concern Ochoa. He was in Cali country, and his good friend Gilberto Rodriguez would get him out quickly. The Cali godfathers knew everything that went on in their stronghold, so they must have been aware that Ochoa was in the area. Yet they made no attempt to get him released.

Ochoa was finally freed on December 30th, but the damage was done and the seeds of distrust were planted. The Medellin godfathers wondered: Did their Cali friends supply the information that got Ochoa arrested? And why didn't they try to get him out of jail quickly?

Meanwhile at his "super cartel" meeting, which included the men from Cali, Escobar laid out his proposal. Under his leadership, the unified cartel would coordinate political and economic strategy for all drug traffickers in Colombia. Moreover, he would not only approve every shipment made, but would get thirty percent of the wholesale value of each one. Two to three years earlier, such a proposal made by the powerful and ruthless bully might have intimidated the Cali godfathers into agreeing to such an outlandish arrangement. According to journalist Simon Strong, when the meeting was over, "Almost speechless with rage, Escobar was reported to have simply muttered, 'But this is war then,' before he immediately left the ranch."

The Cali men were now in a much stronger competing position to reject Escobar's demands categorically and tell the Medellin boss that they would not pay him anything. Indeed, the Cali cartel would now have the wealth to make it possible for it to stand firm against Escobar.

In February 1987, an anonymous letter written in Spanish and postmarked from Cali arrived at the DEA's Miami office. The letter claimed that a shipment of 4,000 kilos of cocaine valued at a mind-boggling $1.7 billion would be arriving in St Petersburg, Florida, aboard a ship named *Amazon Sky*. On April 20th, customs agents boarded the ship to inspect the cargo. One of the cedar boards broke and an agent became suspicious. He got a power drill from his office and drilled into the broken board. Pay dirt! The drill came out tainted with cocaine. They discovered that the boards holding the cocaine were holed out to neatly hide one kilo in each hole.

The authorities decided to stay put. They carefully glued the boards back together and sanded them down to hide the seams. Federal agents knew that the traffickers had been shipping their cocaine in lumber since 1976, but they still marveled at the sophistication of the organization. "You had to look hard to find the seams," Crawford recalled. "It was unbelievable how professional the job was." Tom Cash later estimated that it must have taken an army of about 800 to 1,000 workers to load the boat.

The authorities watched as the *Amazon Sky*'s crew moved the boards over a period of four days to a warehouse complex in St Petersburg. The authorities obtained a search warrant allowing them to videotape the warehouse and wiretap the telephone. Federal agents saw about 700 boards of the cocaine-filled lumber being carried into trucks for the drive to the warehouse. Two weeks after the surveillance began, authorities arrested three men for cocaine smuggling.

But while Pablo fought a two front war with the Cali cartel and Colombian state, the Cali cartel expanded its operations around the world and extending its tentacles deep into Colombia's tottering democracy. With the heat on in Colombia, Cali began to move most of it cocaine-refining operations to Peru and Bolivia and their transportation routes through Venezuela and Central America. The cartel also began muscling into the heroin trade, growing the opium themselves in Colombia and then using their efficient cocaine-distribution network to move the refined product. The heroin the Cali cartel peddled was both purer and cheaper than its chief competitor, the Southeast Asian variety, a good indicator of the brilliance of the Cali cartel godfathers as brilliant criminal businessmen.

In terms of marketing strategy, the alliances the Cali cartel forged with Mexican traffickers were its most important in Latin America. Mexican and Colombian drug traffickers had collaborated on a small scale since the early 1970s, when the Colombian traffickers "piggybacked" their drug loads on smuggling routes that their Mexican counterparts had set up for heroin and marijuana. Still, most of the Colombian cocaine entering the United States from the 1970s through the mid-1980s came by way of the Caribbean.

As the United States stepped up its so-called War on Drugs in the 1980s, law enforcement intensified the pressure on this smuggling corridor, forcing the cartel to seek new routes through Central America and Mexico and across the United States's Southwest border. In reality, the shift was inevitable. Mexico had what the cartel needed – a 2,000-mile expanse of border that offered unlimited smuggling possibilities, experienced smugglers eager to collaborate, and a ready- made infrastructure to meet its needs.

To further its changing distribution strategy, the Cali cartel helped organize a crime federation in Mexico, which consisted of experienced traffickers who could provide safe and reliable smuggling services. According to DEA intelligence, to meet the cartel's transportation needs, "major Mexican traffickers united their operations, which resulted in the formation of a loose federation."

By the early 1990s, sixty to eighty percent of the cocaine

entering the United States came through the Mexican connection, while only twenty to thirty percent continued to be
smuggled via the Caribbean.

The 1989 seizure of more than twenty-one tons in Syl-
mar, California, illustrated how important the Mexican
connection had become in the Cali cartel transportation
scheme of things.

The shipment, at the time the largest cocaine seizure on
record, crossed the Mexican border at El Paso, Texas, and
then was moved by truck to the West Coast. In making the
big bust, law enforcement officials boasted that they had
prevented an even larger amount of cocaine from reaching
the streets, but on further investigation they learned that it
had merely dented the drug smuggling.

`"We realized our encouragement was premature when
we analyzed seized records,"

conceded Tom Constantine, the DEA administrator
from 1994 to 1998. "What we found was even more as-
tounding. We learned that during only a three-month period, the organization had succeeded in smuggling fifty-five
tons of cocaine into the United States. This cocaine had
been trucked to the United States and had already been
distributed on the streets."

Several scenarios have been put forth to explain why the
deteriorating relations erupted into open warfare. One theory popular with many sources is that the two mafias were
locked in a power struggle over the New York market. They

say Cali had dominated the cocaine market since the mid-1970s, but when the market was glutted and prices began to drop in the late 1980s, Medellin's more aggressive element, led by Jose Rodriguez Gacha, started muscling into the lucrative New York market. It is known that Rodriguez Gacha visited New York City in 1988, but other sources say that he went to Queens to mend fences, not to break heads.

Bill Mante, a former New York detective who spent ten years investigating the Cali cartel, believes it was the Medellin cartel's anger at Cali's decision to shift their distribution network to Mexico that led to war. "We can't say for sure, it's purely speculation," Mante said. "But we knew that the Cali cartel had meetings with the Guadalajara cartel about shifting their distribution route to Mexico. That was Jaime Orejuela's brainchild. He had a good relationship with the Mexicans. It was a business decision, but it led to war."

The Colombian government may have tried to encourage the feud. One communiqué from the United States embassy in Bogota to the U.S. State Department stated that General Jaime Ruiz Barrera, commanding general of the Medellin army brigade, and the mayor of Medellin, "are strongly pushing this line, perhaps to keep the cartels at each other's throats."

Roberto Escobar believes that the special relationship the Cali cartel had with the Colombian government was a contributing factor to the war. Roberto wrote in his mem-

oir, *The Accountant's Story* that, "The government never went
after the Cali cartel; instead they were considered Los Ca-
belleros, the gentlemen of the drugs, while we're in Medellin were Los Hampones, the thugs, because we used weapons to protect our property." It was said Pablo liked to fight
but Gilberto liked to pay bribes. Even the head of the DEA
in New York said to the newspapers, "Cali gangs will kill
you if they have to, but they prefer to use a lawyer.'"

But as we explained, the incendiary factor that led to war
was the mutual hatred of drug kingpins Escobar and Pacho
Herrera. The Cali cartel was not going to sit around and
wait for Escobar to make his move. Even before the bombing of Escobar's residence, Edificio Monaco, that tried to
kill Escobar and his family, the Cali cartel was preparing
for war. It began a spy program on Escobar, and it set as
its objective the killing of their nemesis from Medellin.
Cali hired an electronic expert who worked on develop-
ing electronic scanning and locating devices to track the
radio signals of Escobar's mobile phone. The Cali cartel
set up a hideout overlooking Medellin and was able to
intercept calls, record conversations and locate a phone
geographically.

Cali became even more aggressive and hired a group of
hired killers from Medellin known as *Los Briscos*. According to Roberto Escobar, Gilberto Rodriguez Orejuela offered $5 million to the Briscos to kill Pablo, but the leader
of Los Briscos went to Pablo and exposed the plan, and

the group began working for El Patron. In his memoir, Roberto explained, "for Pablo that was also the last evidence he need that the Cali cartel wanted to kill him. So over time, the Cali cartel grew in power as the power of the Medellin cartel declined." From 1984 to 1993, the cartel engaged the Colombian state in a war of attrition, and the terror and death toll that resulted was largely of Pablo Escobar's making.

# CHAPTER FIVE

# THE RUMBLE BEGINS

**W**AR BROKE OUT when the Cali Cartel brazenly bombed Monaco, the luxurious, eight-story apartment building owned by Escobar in the upscale El Poblado barrio in Medellin. Escobar was not home and his family survived. Escobar had no doubt who was responsible. He sent hit squads to Cali and launched a series of bombing attacks against the drug store chain owned by Gilberto Rodriguez. All that did, though, was kill innocent customers of the drugstore and residents in the neighborhood, but the war of the cartels was on.

Figuring that the best defense is good offense, the Cali godfathers did not let up. They sent their own hit squads to Cali. A week after the Cali cartel dispatched a team of assassins, their body parts were delivered to Cali. The mission was incompetently directed by Cali cartel associate Major Gomez. Strangers in Medellin during this tense time were bound to attract attention, especially when they drove around Escobar's neighborhood bearing Cali license tags. But this is what the Cali cartel hit squad had done.

Despite the botched mission, Major Gomez thought he was safe in Cali from Escobar, but few could escape El Patron's wrath. Soon after the major had sent his hit men to Medellin, he drove to his office in his bullet proof car. When he arrived, he got out of his car and walked the short distance to his office building. This particular morning a dump trunk blocked the entrance. Halfway between the car and his office, five men armed with M16s stood up in the truck's bed and opened fire, killing Gomez. The killers vanished without a trace.

Escobar also sent hit men to Cali to detonate a car bomb at a location that Miguel Rodriguez was supposed to pass on the way to his office. But the bomb exploded prematurely killing the two hit men and demolishing three houses in Miguel's neighborhood. Miguel was actually home and heard the blast, even though it was half a mile away

In the following months, the casualties inexorably mounted. On July 11th, authorities discovered the bodies of five ex-military men outside Medellin with a note explaining that the mercenaries were killed because they were *sicarios* for the Cali cartel. Three weeks later, police captured Jose Luis Gavria, Escobar's cousin and charged him with participating in the killings. On August 18th, arsonists torched the biggest Medellin outlet of Gilberto Rodriguez's Drogas

La Rebaja chain of drug stores. In mid-August, Colombian military intelligence officials reported that sixty members of the Cali cartel and eighteen members of the Medellin cartel had been killed since the Monaco bombing.

The U.S. embassy noted in a cable that "their intelligence against each other appears to be very good, especially that of the Medellin cartel against the Cali cartel." Both sides realized that war was bad for the drug business and tried to negotiate a truce, but there was too much bad blood. "They tried to meet several times, but it never happened," revealed Javier Pena, a retired DEA agent who played a major role in the hunt for Pablo Escobar. "They were just too big for the same territory."

Instead of working toward peace, the two mafias got increasingly vicious in their attacks. One 200-pound bomb planted inside a Renault exploded outside a Rebaja outlet in Cali, killing seven people, wounding twenty-four more, destroying a supermarket and damaging twenty other business and seven houses.

The war spread to the United States, and, in the last week of August, the media reported on several dozen bombings in New York and Miami. According to the *New York Times*, law enforcement officials were saying that, "There was evidence that the two cartels. . . had begun informing the police about each other's shipments" and that, "as a result of the anonymous tips, police made several large seizures during the year." The Cali cartel also sent more than ten professional killers to the United States from Colombia, according to the *New York Times*. New York City officials worried that their city would experience the same kind of out-of-control violence that ravaged Miami in the late 1970s and early 1980s.

Both cartels went even further and hired foreign mercenaries. Yair Klein, a retired Israeli defense Force colonel, helped arrange a shipment of 100 Uzi submachine guns, 460 Galil automatic rifles and 200,000 rounds of ammunition to Medellin cartel kingpin Rodriguez Gacha, and trained some of his men, including his son Freddy. The weapons were manufactured in Israel and believed to be a part of a shipment sold legally in 1988 by state-owned Israeli Military Industries to the Government of Antigua. The Antiguan authorities said they never ordered the arms for their defense force, which numbered just ninety personnel. They were later able to determine that the guns had been off-loaded from a Danish ship to another ship at an Antiguan port in 1989 and then smuggled to Colombia. An Israeli bank had financed the deal.

Yair Klein was a former lieutenant in the Israeli army, who, in the 1980s, established a paramilitary company named Sparhead Ltd, which he used to funnel guns and provide training in South America. He was accused of training cartel sicarios and of involvement in the infamous 1989 Avianca airline bombing ordered by Pablo Escobar. It was also suspected that some of his weapons were used to assassinate Luis Carlos Galan, a leading Colombian presidential candidate, in 1989.

The Colombian authorities charged Klein and several former Israeli officers with providing arms and training to drug traffickers. Klein denied the charges, but in 1991 an Israel court convicted him of exporting arms to Colombia and fined him $13,400. In early 1991, a U.S. Senate Governmental Permanent Subcommittee strongly criticized Israel for Klein's role in arming and training Rodriguez Gacha and other Medellin cartel leaders. The Committee charged that Israel knew what Klein was doing in Colombia, but it took no action until after media publicized Klein's activities.

It took another seven years before the Colombians officially indicted Klein. One of the major pieces of evidence against him was a training video used to instruct death squads.

That did not stop Klein from arms smuggling and paramilitary activities. In January 1999, years after his involvement in the Colombian cartel war, he was arrested in a war torn Sierra Leone on suspicion of supplying and training rebels. Klein claimed to be in Africa looking for diamond mines. The Sierra Leone government did not extradite Klein to Colombia; instead, Reuben Gross, a Israeli parking garage magnate nicknamed the "Parking King," helped to obtain his release. Klein promptly disappeared.

But Klein could not avoid trouble with the law. Klein

spent 16 months in the Sierra Leone prison system on charges of smuggling arms to rebels from the Revolutionary United Front (RUF). In 2001, Klein was convicted in absentia in a Colombian court on charges of conspiracy to form a paramilitary group and sentenced him to ten years in prison.

An arrest warrant was issued for Klein's arrest in 2007 on charges of conspiracy to train a terrorist group. When he was arrested in Russia, Colombia made an extradition request for fear that he would be in danger if locked up in a Colombian prison. Instead, Russia sent him to Israel in exchange for a Russian who had been arrested in Israel. No one expected the Israelis to hand over the mercenary to Colombian authorities.

Meanwhile Klein called the international arrest warrant "complete nonsense" and announced plans to begin writing books. At this writing, the Colombian government is still trying to enforce the guilty verdict of Yair Klein, the mercenary who played a prominent role in the war of the cartels.

The Cali Cartel brought in Jorge Salcedo to oversee its security work. Codenamed "Richard" by the Cali cartel, Salcedo became an important member of the Cali cartel's intelligence and security team and typical of the type of talented employee the cartel liked to hire. The son of a retired brigadier general in the Colombian armed forces, Salcedo had studied economics and mechanical engineering in the United States and was fluent in English. After joining the military, he became a member of the Brigade of Cali, where he acquired expertise in arms, communications and explosives. He distinguished himself in the fight against M-19 guerrillas during the 1980s, until the group disbanded and integrated itself into Colombian society.

Through his contacts in the Cali-based Third Brigade, Salcedo became good friends with Mario del Basto, the Cali cartel's head of security. Salcedo had excellent skills, including knowledge of computers and the cartel recruited him. Salcedo eventually became a trusted intimate of the Rodriguez brothers. DEA agents who later worked with Salcedo described him as cultured, highly intelligent, charismatic and remarkably cool under pressure.

In August 1988, Salcedo devised a plan to bring in a team of British mercenaries to kill Escobar. Salcedo's contact was the British mercenary David Tomkins. To develop the plan, Salcedo went to London to meet with Tomkins and his partner Robert Peter McAleese.

Before he became a mercenary, Tompkins had been in and out of jail since the 1960s. Tomkins mercenary career began in Africa, and over the years, his thirst for adventure took his all over the world, from Afghanistan to Croatia to Uganda where he was involved in a plot to kill Idi Amin. In Angola, Tomkins became one of the famous "Dogs of War" and an explosives expert under the notorious mercenary leader, Colonel Callan.

Born in Scotland, McAleese was a former British paratrooper and former member of the SAS, who left the British military to become a mercenary. McAleese had also seen extensive action in Africa. After suffering a serious parachuting accident, he returned to the United Kingdom when he hooked up with Tompkins.

Before his meeting with Salcedo, Tomkins had been drawn into the Colombian civil war when he met a Colombian army officer through a contact in the arms trade. The officer asked him to recruit a team of mercenaries that could destroy the headquarters of Colombia's FARC guerilla group. At the time, FARC was involved in a death struggle with the Colombia's drug cartels over control of the narcotics trade. The operation was essentially funded by Medellin drug lord Jose Gonzalo Rodriguez Gauche. Tomkins was to be paid about $2,000 a week, plus he could keep any loot he found at FARC headquarters. Tomkins teamed up with McAleese to recruit a 16-man mercenary team and then headed for Colombia.

After meeting in a London bar to plan, Rodriguez Gacha funded the operation. Salcedo assured Tomkins and McAleese that they would not have to worry about the Colombian government, and they were promised luxurious accommodations in a villa near Cali, as well as a substantial budget to buy weapons.

After arriving in Cali, the team was instructed to keep a low profile and to try and act like tourists. Easier said than done. The team began frequenting a bar run by an expatriate, and, soon, their visits led to arguments and drunken brawls. Salcedo moved the mercenaries to a secluded ranch owned by Miguel Rodriguez Orejuela. In this quieter setting, the Tomkins team trained regularly while they awaited orders. The plan was to launch a helicopter attack on Hacienda Napoles, Escobar's 7,000 acre private estate, located about 80 miles from Medellin. The mercenaries planned to launch the mission when they knew Escobar would be at his ranch. It was a bold mission. To reach Hacienda Napoles from Cali, the mercenaries would have to travel three hours across thick jungle.

Meanwhile, the Cali cartel was hard at work trying to track the radio signal of Escobar's mobile phone. The cartel positioned a team of spies in a hideout overlooking Medellin where they attempted to intercept Escobar's mobile phone signals. On May 31, 1989, the spies sent word back to their leaders in Cali that Escobar would be for sure at Hacienda Napoles to celebrate his soccer team's victory in Copa Liberadores de America. It was the first time a Colombian team had on the tournament in 41 years.

A pair of Vietnam era Huey helicopters painted to look like police choppers were readied. Tompkins and his team were worried that one of the Hueys would have difficulty carrying the commandos and munitions to the drop zone. But Gilberto Rodriguez Orejuela was insistent that the Brit mercenaries launched the mission, which became known as Operation Phoenix. The spy team arranged for someone to call Escobar promptly at 11 am. The person had to hear Escobar's voice or the mission was off. When the caller confirmed that Escobar was at the ranch, the four former Cali cartel godfathers, who were back in Cali, monitoring live reports from the scene, cheered.

The mission, however, was in trouble. Near the drug zone, the Huey carrying the heavy load was low on fuel. The mission, moreover, could not handle the topography and weather. The 8,000 foot mountain range and the heavy clouds blocked the pilots' view of the range and the plane crashed.

The pilot died, but, miraculously, Tomkins and MacAleese survived. When no help came from Cali, the two men spent three days walking out of the jungle and evading capture and death, even though they were in the heart of Escobar country. McAleese suffered broken ribs and a sprained back, Tompkins, mere bruises. In June 1989, Tompkins returned home to the United Kingdom via Panama. The Cali cartel still hoped to kill Escobar at Hacienda Napoles, but the Colombian authorities eventually seized the ranch and Escobar could not go there.

Always the adventurer and risk taker, Tomkins was still keen on killing Escobar. Tomkins told a Colombian reporter, "Right now, we have three choices: run, hide or go ahead, There is nowhere to run and we can't hide. So we are determined to go on until we finish what we came here to do."

In 1991, Tomkins once again became involved with a

"Get Escobar" scheme, when U.S authorities claimed a drug gang (not the Cali cartel) offered him to do the deed. The plot was to involve a Vietnam-era fighter jet and 500 pound bombs. U.S. Customs agents in Puerto Rico discovered the plot and set up an undercover sting in which Tompkins handed over $25,000 to undercover agents in return for what Tompkins thought would be a shipment of arms. Before he was arrested, Tomkins was tipped off, and he fled back to the United Kingdom. In 1994, Tomkins was indicted in the Southern District of Florida for conspiracy to violate arms export laws.

McAleese managed to avoid trouble with the law, and in the mid 1990s he went to work training Russian bodyguards in Moscow and later security work in Algeria and Iraq. McAleese remained free until 2003 when U.S. Customs arrested him at the Houston International Airport as he tried to enter the country. McAleese had traveled to the U.S. to attend survival training courses at Fort Bliss, Texas, with plans to travel to Iraq where he would help with the war against terrorism.

It was not be the last time that the Medellin and Cali cartels would go outside the country seeking aide in their war to the death. In September 1991, Salcedo met with Roberto Leyva, a colonel in El Salvador's air force. Arriving in El Salvador, Salcedo posed as an entrepreneur who wanted to invest in the country and was looking for partners. Leyva was interested in what Salcedo had to propose, since he was about to retire from the air force and wanted to make some money. Salcedo and the colonel hit it off and became friends.

Three months went by before Salcedo told his friend the real reason why he had come to El Salvador. He represented an officer in the Colombian military who worried about the Colombian guerrillas' growing power, Salcedo explained, and he wanted to find some bombs that the officer could use against the guerrillas. "Could you help out, Colonel?" Salcedo asked. "We don't expect a decision right now. Let's meet in the New Year."

Salcedo and Leyva met again on January 7th at the Hotel Charleston in El Salvador. This time, Salcedo came prepared to tell the truth. He was actually representing the Cali cartel, he told Leyva, which was urgently looking for bombs that it could use to destroy the jail where Pablo Escobar was imprisoned. The cartel emissary laid out the operation's main details. They planned to use a UH-212 helicopter to carry a bomb and drop it on Escobar's jail.

"We are willing to pay four million dollars for the bombs," Salcedo said.

"I can get the bombs," the colonel assured him. They agreed to meet again in San Salvador.

The details of what happened next remain a mystery, but authorities know for certain that the cartel and its associates in El Salvador flew three of the four bombs out of the country from a remote coastal airstrip. However, Salvadorian agents foiled the plot, arresting nine people, including some Salvadorian air force members, and seizing one of the bombs and almost $400,000 in cash. By this time, Escobar was in jail and to protect Escobar against possible future aerial attack, Colombian authorities mounted aircraft guns at the Cathedral and banned air traffic over the complex.

The experience of the cartels with foreign mercenaries showed that they would go to any length to destroy each other. The problem—the plots always seemed to fail and the war subsequently dragged on with no sign of victory for either side.

Gilberto Rodriguez.

Miguel Rodriguez.

Jose Santacruz.

Pacho Herrera.

The four drug lords of the Cali cartel. Gilberto was known as the Chess Player for this calculation and strategy. Miguel was the hands-on micro-manager. Santacruz, rugged and low key, was the most violent of the group, while the dapper Herrera was the stereotypical sharp-suited drug trafficker.
(Photos supplied by the DEA)

An aerial view of the site of the Minden explosion in upstate New York, with the wrecked laboratory in the top left corner, which led to a concerted investigation of the Cali cartel. *(DEA)*

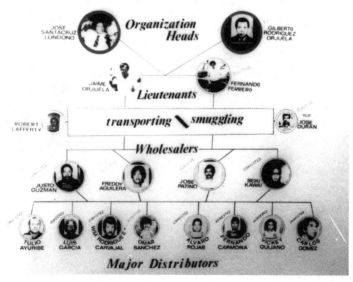

An early organisational chart of the Santacruz Londono organization. The Cali men made New York City their early base. *(DEA)*

A smiling Chepe Santacruz with his wife and children, looking every inch the successful businessman and devoted father. *(DEA)*

One of Chepe's opulent residences, with obligatory swimming pool, in Cali. The mafia made untold billions of dollars and bought numerous properties in their native Colombia. *(DEA)*

Pablo Escobar, dubbed "the World's Greatest Outlaw."

Harold Ackerman, Cali cartel 'ambassador' to the U.S., became a witness against his bosses after being sentenced to six life terms. (DEA)

What $2 million looks like: the first major money hit against the cartel after Miguel Rodriguez had taken control, seized after a high-speed chase across New York's George Washington Bridge. (From left) Ken Spiro, Everett Pearsall, Bob Odell, Bill Mante, Frank Diaz, Mike Reeves and Captain John Burns. (New York State Police)

Jose Gonzalo Gacha in football strip. A close ally of Pablo Escobar, the Medellin trafficker was tracked by his enemies in Cali and shot dead by Colombian security forces in 1989. *(DEA)*

The corpulent body of Pablo Escobar. The brutal leader of the Medellin cartel waged war against both the Colombian state and the Cali mob until he was gunned down on a rooftop. (DEA)

General Rosso José Serrano, the studious
but tough police commander who drove
the fight against the men from Cali.

Ernesto Samper, the Colombian President
accused by the U.S. of accepting Cali
money for his election campaign.
*(Ernesto Samper)*

Andres Pastrana Arango,
former president of
Colombia who received
the narco cassettes

Gilberto Rodriguez being booked after his capture in June 1995. "Don't shoot, I'm a man of peace," he told his captors. *(DEA)*

Agents posing with Miguel Rodriguez, who was caught just two months after his brother: (left to right) Dave Mitchell, Chris Feistl, CNP Colonel Gomez, Jerry Salameh and Ruben Prieto. *(DEA)*

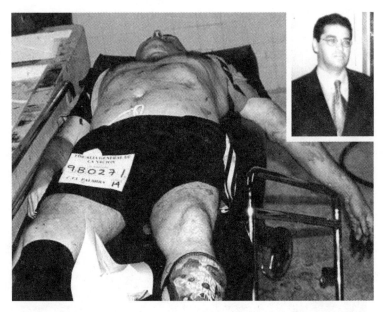

The dapper Pacho Herrera dressed like a *GQ* model (inset) but was shot dead while playing a football match in prison in a hit organized by a rival trafficker. *(Reuters)*

Gilberto Rodriguez, aged 65, is escorted by Colombian soldiers to a flight to Miami after his extradition to face serious drug charges in December 2004. *(Associated Press)*

# CHAPTER SIX

# A WAR OF ATTRITION

**A**S THE WAR dragged on, the attitude of Colombia's security forces increasingly frustrated and angered Escobar. From Escobar's perspective, the Colombian government seemed interested only in taking down his cartel, not the one in Cali, and he suspected that the security forces were in bed with his bitter rivals.

Rumors circulated that Escobar believed Gilberto Rodriguez had worked out a deal with the DEA. There were good signs that Escobar was right. In April 1988, for example, Colombian General Ruiz told the press that Escobar was plotting to eliminate the top members of the Cali cartel, but he failed to mention the similar plan the Cali men had for Escobar and his associates.

Later, former Colombian officials confirmed what Escobar suspected, but made no apology for focusing their attention and resources on him and his Medellin associates.

"We viewed Escobar and the Medellin cartel as the worst of two evils," explained Cesar Gaviria Trujillo, the president of Colombia from 1988 to 1992, and former the president of the Organization of American States. "That's why the Colombian government directed all its attention and resources against the Medellin cartel."

"The DEA office in Colombia had to follow the Colombian government's lead," said Joe Toft, a retired DEA agent who joined the agency's office in Bogota in 1988. "We were concerned about the Cali cartel, of course," Toft said. "We had agents working on both cartels, and the group assigned to the Cali cartel worked just as hard as the Medellin group. But the Colombian government's focus was on Medellin, which had declared war on the state. So we couldn't get the Colombian government to do much on Cali."

As the War of the Cartels dragged on, Escobar continued to see plenty of evidence documenting the collusion. In June 1989, for example, police seized government documents from former army captain Luis Javier Wanomen and Jose Rivera, a civilian, showing that two top government officials, Raul Orejuela, the interior minister, and Colonel Oscar Pelaez, director of the F-2 intelligence agency, were collaborating with the Cali cartel by passing on information from agencies staffed by high-level Colombian officials.

The Colombian government could have cared less about such revelations, so Escobar decided to take care of his problems. He targeted Miguel Masa, the head of DAS

(Administrative Department of Security), Colombia's equivalent of the FBI, whom he believed was on the Cali payroll. Escobar flooded the streets with leaflets, offering $1.3 million for Masa's head.

When Escobar seethed, Colombia shivered. On 25 May 1989, a 220-pound car bomb exploded near a convoy carrying Masa and his bodyguards through downtown Bogota, killing six people and injuring more than fifty. Three months later, Escobar and his allies elevated their terror campaign to another level, murdering leading presidential candidate Luis Carlos Galan, despite his sixteen bodyguards.

Many Colombians believed the charismatic Galan would win the 1990 election and continued Barco's tough policy toward drug trafficking. His death was a turning point, as the Colombian government went all out to take down Escobar. Using his powers under the state of siege, Barco reinstated the U.S.–Colombia extradition treaty, which the Colombian courts had suspended and launched an all-out war against the Medellin cartel. Between mid-August and mid-December 1989, the government arrested 497 people, seized $250 million in drugs and property, and extradited nine suspects to the United States. Escobar struck back during the same period, killing 187 officials and civilians, carrying out 205 bombings, and causing $501 million in damage. The terror blitz culminated in two spectacular attacks.

On November 27<sup>th</sup>, Dandenny Munoz-Mosquera (nicknamed "Tyson"), a Medellin *sicario* believed responsible for killing fifty police officers, judges and other officials, arranged to have a bomb planted aboard Avianca's Flight 203, en route from Bogota to Medellin. The plane exploded over Bogota, killing all 107 passengers aboard, including two Americans.

The "official" explanation of the bombing was that Escobar wanted two informants on board the plane dead, but sources revealed that the shocking incident happened because Escobar wanted to kill a girlfriend of Miguel Rodriguez, who was on board, in revenge for the bomb blast that partially deafened his daughter Manuela. The flight was due to take less than an hour over partially mountainous terrain. When the plane reached 13,000 feet, an explosion ripped through the cabin, causing a fire on the plane's right side. A second explosion blew the plane apart, showering the ground with wreckage over a three-mile radius.

The investigation focused on one man: Dandenny Munoz-Mosquera, who was believed to be Escobar's chief assassin. According to intelligence reports, Munoz-Mosquera started working for Escobar at age twelve, and by his teens, he was running a school for *sicarios* that trained poor children from the city's slums. Munoz-Mosquera was quickly captured, but he escaped twice. In September 1991, U.S. authorities received word that he suspect had somehow slipped into the U.S. and was hiding in Queens. New

York. Acting on a tip, DEA agents staked out a phone booth. When Munoz-Mosquera showed up, the agents arrested him.

Munoz-Mosquera was charged with carrying false identification and lying to federal authorities. The feds told the judge that the young Colombian was a violent criminal responsible for many deaths in Colombia and they needed time to build a solid case against him. The judge gave Munoz-Mosquera the maximum sentence of six years. In the summer of 1992, a federal grand jury indicted Munoz-Mosquera on thirteen counts of murder, drug trafficking, racketeering and terrorism.

The basis for the arrest was an obscure 1986 law that allowed the U.S. to prosecute for terrorist acts against its citizens abroad. Pablo Escobar, the suspected mastermind of the Avianca bombing and now a fugitive, was named a co-defendant. As the authorities prepared their case against Munoz-Mosquera, they received a word that the defendant was planning a prison escape and talked about killing Cheryl Pollack, the case's prosecutor. She was given round-the-clock protection. It took two trials to convict Munoz-Mosquera, even though, as part of its prosecution, the U.S. presented 20 so-called cooperating witnesses, associates for Pablo Escobar, who, it said, could tie Munoz Mosquera to the Avianca bombing.

In the first trial, two jurors did not believe the witnesses. In the second trial, the jury found him guilty on all thirteen counts. Allowed to address the court before sentencing, Munoz-Mosquera said, "I'd just like to say that God and the government know I'm innocent. Thank you very much. God bless you." The judge gave the defendant ten consecutive life sentences, plus 45 years.

Was Munoz-Mosquera responsible for the heinous Avianca bombing? The evidence shows that Munoz-Mosquera was a vicious assassin, but former Colombian government officials raised doubts about his responsibility for the bombing. Questions have also been raised as to whether he got a fair trial; it is suspected that the Munoz-Mosquera case was one of several in which the FBI mishandled evidence and distorted testimony.

A U.S. Inspector General's report suggested that "unqualified FBI agents, working in the FBI's lab, were under pressure to make the lab results fit the theory of how the crime was perpetrated." In other words, the government broke the rules in its march to prosecution. Today, Munoz-Mosquera is incarcerated in the maximum security prison at Florence, Colorado. For company, he has such notorious criminals as Ted Kacyznski, the Unibomber; Ramzi Yousef, the terrorist responsible for the first World Trade Center bombing in 1993, and many others. He will never again see the light of day.

Meanwhile, the war of the cartels continued. Another bomb in December outside the headquarters of DAS killed fifty-two people, injured 1,000, gouged a thirty foot- deep crater and damaged buildings forty blocks away. It was the biggest narco-terrorist attack in Colombian history.

The Cali cartel retaliated, showing that spies and intelligence information could be more effective than outright carnage. In early 1989, the cartel leadership hired Jorge Enrique Velasquez, nicknamed "The Navigator," to infiltrate the organization of Jose Gonzalo Rodriguez Gacha. Velasquez did such a good job that Rodriguez Gacha entrusted him totally with his security. "The Cali cartel paid Velasquez a million dollars to get the Mexican," said Pena. "Velasquez led the police right to Rodriguez Gacha."

Rodriguez Gacha learned that the police knew he was hiding at his ranch near Tolu, some sixty miles south of the coastal town of Cartagena, but he suspected son Freddy, not Velasquez, as unintentionally being the source of the lead. *No problem*, Rodriguez Gacha figured. He had an escape route.

Unfortunately for the trafficker, he shared it with The Navigator, who gave it up to the police. On 15 December 1989, security forces killed Rodriguez Gacha, son Freddy, and several bodyguards in a shootout.

The Mexican was dead, but the war and carnage continued. In March 1990, bombs exploded in Cali, Bogota, and Medellin simultaneously, killing twenty-six people and injuring 200 more. Escobar increased the bounty he was willing to pay for the killing of a police officer to $4,000, plus a bonus of $8,000 for the killing of any member of the security forces. Within three months, 108 policemen had been murdered.

By 1990, President Barco had spent four years trying to bring Escobar down, but the drug lord remained on the loose and narco-terrorism was still a way of life in the country. That May, Cesar Gaviria Trujillo won the presidential election, becoming the youngest president in Colombian history. Gaviria had begun his political career by winning election to Congress at age twenty-five, and one year later was mayor of Pereira, his hometown in the coffee-growing region. While climbing the political ladder, Gaviria gained a reputation as a competent technocrat, and he served in the Barco administration, first as minister of finance (1986–1987) and then as minister of the interior (1987–1989).

In 1989, he left the government to manage the presidential campaign of Senator Luis Carlos Galan. After Galan's shocking assassination, the Liberal party selected Gaviria as their presidential candidate. His campaign stressed a get-tough platform that granted no concessions to the traffickers. Once in office, however, Gaviria did an about-face and began pursuing a policy of compromise rather than confrontation.

On August 7th, Gaviria made a generous offer to the drug barons: turn yourself in and you will receive light sentences and immunity from extradition. Escobar sensed weakness and increased the pressure on the government to wring more concessions from Gaviria. In September, he kidnapped journalist Francisco Santos, a member of the family that owned *El Tiempo*, the country's largest newspaper, and Marina Montoya, the sister of German Montoya, former secretary of the presidency. Escobar shrewdly concluded that making the country's elite a major target of his terror campaign was the best way to change the government policy.

On September 25th, Escobar renewed his two-front war with a bold attack at an estate outside Cali near Candaleria, reputedly owned by the Rodriguez brothers. Eighteen people were killed and several others wounded. The CNP later captured four men who confessed that Tyson Munoz-Mosquera had hired them to make the attack.

The wave of kidnappings and killings continued into late October. The Cali cartel sent two men and a woman to Bogota to carry out hits on Medellin targets, but they were captured, gagged with their feet and hands bound, wrapped in mattresses, and tortured before each was shot fifteen times. Before fleeing, the killers sprayed the scene of the crime with slogans: "Death to the Cali Cartel," "Here are three killers from Cali," and "War is war, and, if you do not believe it, look at the bodies."

In another incident, twelve men were hauled from their rooms in a hotel in Medellin. Four of them were found shot to death, while the other eight remained missing. Two of the dead had signs pinned on their bodies that read, "Because they are from the Cali Cartel." War is war."

Authorities predicted the war of the cartels would get uglier. A few weeks after the kidnappings of Francisco Santos and Marina Montoya, Gaviria issued the first of two decrees giving further concessions to the drug traffickers. Now, all a trafficker had to do when he surrendered was confess to just one crime and he would avoid extradition if any new charges were brought after the surrender. Escobar responded by offering another carrot – the release of three hostages.

President Gaviria issued a third decree in December, offering traffickers "full judicial benefits" if they confessed to a single crime. The Ochoa brothers were the ones who finally took the government's offer. The deal was simply too good to turn down. Serve a few years in jail, with no possibility of being extradited to the United States, and they could get out and still have their fortunes to spend.

On December 17th, Fabio Ochoa, accompanied by his mother and sisters, surrendered to authorities at a church located about twenty kilometers south of Medellin. "I feel the same happiness entering jail as someone else feels when leaving it," Fabio told the press. "I only wanted to end the nightmare of my life." Following their brother's lead, Jorge surrendered the next month and Juan David in February.

With Rodriguez Gacha dead and the Ochoas in jail, Escobar was now alone in his two-front war. He feared extradition if he turned himself in, for there was no guarantee that he would get the same concessions as the Ochoas. After all, he had not stopped murdering and kidnapping after Gaviria had issued his first decree. In the end, he continued fighting the state the only way he knew how: narco-terrorism. In January, Marina Montoya's body was found in Bogota with six bullets in her head.

During a raid near Medellin, police accidently killed another of Escobar's kidnapped victims, Diane Turbay, the offspring of another prominent Colombian family and the daughter of a former presidential candidate. Gaviria sensed that Colombians were tired of living under the siege of narco-terrorism, and he continued to pursue the surrender policy he had sweetened and proposed to the traffickers. He issued a fourth decree guaranteeing immunity from extradition for all offenses committed from the date of surrender and not just from the first decree.

Meanwhile, in early 1991, as part of its effort to reform the country's constitution, the Constitutional Assembly debated its extradition policy, giving consideration to banning it completely. Since 1984, the extradition treaty had been used to send at least forty-nine suspected drug traffickers to the United States. *The Extraditables*, an unidentified group opposed to the extradition of Colombian nationals to other countries for trial, released a statement in Bogota, saying that the recent killings of Turbay and Montoya were not meant to intimidate the Constitutional Assembly and "respectfully requesting that extradition be prohibited by the new constitution." Escobar freed the last of his kidnapped victims as part of his clever campaign to bring Colombia to its knees.

The vote on extradition was never in doubt. Reports were rampant that the drug traffickers had bribed and intimidated the Constitutional Assembly. One of its members, Augusto Ramirez, collaborated with the police and arranged for one of Escobar's lawyers to offer him 4,000 pesos while police filmed the exchange. The lawyer told Ramirez that Escobar had given him the money and that thirty-nine other members had already taken the same amount.

The drug traffickers threatened those members of the Constitutional Assembly who could not be bought off. Juan Carlos Esguerra, later a foreign minister in the Ernesto Samper administration, received a letter reminding him what had happened to others who supported extradition.

The list included such names as Luis Carlos Galan, Guillermo Cano and Diane Turbay, a "who's who" of assassinated Colombians. "The cartels put a lot of pressure on us," Esguerra recalled. "It wasn't just the Medellin cartel. The Cali cartel spread its money around and its lawyers were always hanging around during the debate on extradition."

In 1997, Guillermo Pallomari, who worked for the Cali cartel as its head accountant from 1990 to 1994, testified that the Cali cartel set up a "structure" of bribes and payoffs to the Constitutional Assembly through Mario Ramirez, the secretary of the Assembly. According to Pallomari, Ramirez "had the task of contacting members of the Constitutional Assembly to relay to them the wishes of the Cali cartel regarding various laws, including the new extradition law."

The cartel also had its house lawyers working hard to influence the extradition vote. In 1989, Miguel Rodriguez directed Michael Abbell to draft and forward a memorandum to be used in Colombia. It included a comparative study of standards of extradition then existing in U.S. treaties with various countries in South America.

The following year, Miguel had Abbell draft and forward a memorandum to a Colombian congressman, which contained language prohibiting the extradition of Colombia nationals in the proposed redrafted constitution. In effect, the Cali cartel was trying to rewrite the constitution. In late November 1991, a Cali courier delivered $86,000 to a member of the Constitutional Assembly for his work in nullifying the extradition treaty.

Despite the intense pressure, Esguerra voted for extradition, even though President Cesar Gaviria provided little support. "One could see where the [Gaviria] administration stood on the extradition issue," Esquerra recalled. "No one represented the government when it came time for the Assembly to debate. That made it difficult for those members who wanted to support extradition."

Carlos Lemos, later Colombia's vice president during the Samper presidency, was another Assembly member who voted for extradition. "Members were afraid," Lemos recalled. "The cartels had too many resources – money, guns – at their disposal and too much influence. The vote was never in doubt." The vote was fifty-one against extradition and thirteen for, with ten abstentions.

Pablo Escobar never doubted the outcome either. In late May, he had announced he would give himself up in exchange for the promise from President Gaviria that he would be treated leniently and not extradited to the United States, where he faced at least ten indictments for drug trafficking and murder. The drug lord now had everything he wanted. It was time to turn himself in and join the Ochoas in jail.

On 19 June 1991, the most wanted man in Colombia – perhaps the world – was picked up from an undisclosed location and flown to his hometown of Envigado, where he was incarcerated in a plush prison especially built for him. Wearing military fatigues and dark glasses, Escobar was accompanied by Father Rafael Gavria Herreros, an eighty-two-year-old Roman Catholic priest who had mediated the godfather's surrender. When the helicopter arrived at its destination, Escobar fell on his knees before Father Gavria Herreros and begged the priest for his blessing.

The Colombian people breathed a collective sigh of relief. They were exhausted by all the killing, the fear, and the destructions. They believed that narco-terrorism had ended with Escobar's surrender and that there would be peace in their time. In a poll held close to the extradition vote of the Constitutional Assembly, eighty-two percent of Colombians said they opposed extradition.

While Escobar warred with the state, the Cali cartel continued to grow in power, wealth and reach, solidifying its U.S. base and expanding into Europe and Latin America. By 1990, U.S. officials, who, a few months earlier, said that the Medellin cartel was responsible for most of the cocaine smuggled into the United States, now revealed that the Cali syndicate had grabbed the lion's share of the traffic.

"Precise figures are difficult to ascertain, but a little more than a year ago, the Medellin cartel was believed to be responsible for about seventy-five percent of the cocaine shipments to the United States and Europe," Douglas Farah, a reporter with the *Washington Post*, wrote in 1990. "Now, say officials, Medellin's share is below fifty percent."

`The Cali share of the U.S. market had jumped to around seventy percent, according to U.S. officials, and they estimated that it now controlled ninety percent of the European cocaine market. In a July 1991 issue, *Time* magazine devoted nine pages to "The New Leaders of Coke," centered on a lengthy interview with Gilberto Rodriguez himself. The avuncular drug baron had consented to meet two reporters as part of a charm offensive – *Time* called it "a nine-hour public relations blitz" – designed to portray himself as both a legitimate businessman and an innocent target of the 'psychopathic' Escobar.

As a white-coated butler offered a variety of beverages

and a secretary took verbatim notes, the reporters noted that the Chess Player's curly black hair was now flecked with white and he had gained at least thirty pounds in the past few years. His *élan*, however, was undiminished. Dressed casually in a pink-striped cotton shirt and dark trousers – offset by a thick gold crucifix on a neck chain, a gold-and steel Cartier watch, and his small, manicured hands – Gilberto denied any involvement in drug trafficking and protested that if the authorities ever arrested him, Escobar would have him killed. He labeled his Medellin rival "sick, a psycho, a lunatic. He knows he's lost the war against the state. He lives now only to destroy."

He blamed the conflict on Escobar's tendency to see anyone who did not back him as an enemy. "All this started when Mr. Escobar called me and asked me to help him commit violent acts to get the Colombian government to abrogate the 1979 [extradition] treaty. Mr. Escobar thinks that one must take justice into one's own hands. I don't agree. He thinks that a criminal can win a war against the state. I think that is absurd. The crimes he has committed in Colombia on the pretext of narco trafficking have been very grave mistakes."

Rodriguez dismissed the Cali cartel as "a poor invention" of General Jaime Ruiz. "He chased Mr. Escobar and his partners persistently and yet failed in all his attempts. He didn't succeed in gaining immortality with the Medellin cartel. Thus the Cali cartel was invented, and with it the war over the New York market. Of course, this tale about the Cali cartel has been helped along by my differences with Mr Escobar."

Even though Escobar was in jail, he was still trying to kill him, Rodriguez claimed. So he continued to take extraordinary security measures, such as dividing his time between six or seven houses in Cali, not spending Christmas with his seven grown children, and having to celebrate the birthdays of family members on the wrong days.

For all the smooth bravura of his performance, the Chess Player must have been nervous. Like many other Colombians, he must have doubted that Escobar would stay in prison and pay his debt to society.

# CHAPTER SEVEN

# EXIT EL PATRON

**T**O ATTACK THE powerful drug cartels, the Colombian government organized the Bloque de Busqueda (Search Block), a combined police-army-marine antinarcotics force of 1,500 personnel, which had received training from the United States. In reality, Pablo Escobar was the only drug trafficker that Search Block seemed interested in pursuing. In his typical style of always going on the offensive, Escobar tried to relieve the heat by putting a $27,000 bounty on each Search Block member.

By now, the Colombian public was wondering if El Patron had been protected by Divine Intervention. His exploits during his years on the run had made him a legend in Colombia, and even while in prison, he remained the King of Cocaine. Like the proverbial cat with too many lives, Escobar had escaped time and again, often dramatically, as he stayed one step ahead of his relentless pursuers. Sometimes

Search Block would get so close that Escobar had to use such clever disguises or tactics to flee, such as dressing as a woman or riding in a coffin in a carriage.

His legend grew as the press reported on the drug lord's "imprisonment." Indeed, Colombians began to wonder if he was really the jailer. "It is a prison that's no better than any for a similar criminal in the United States," President Gaviria assured his countrymen. "I do not think any of us would like to spend time there."

Cynical Colombians scoffed, and dubbed the prison holding Escobar "La Catedral" – the Cathedral. Escobar's new home stood high on a hill, part of a ten-acre spread that included a soccer field, a gymnasium, a recreational center, a discotheque, a bar and a sweeping view of the Medellin Valley below. Don Pablo, in fact, had supervised the prison's construction. His 1,000-square-foot "cell" was bigger than the warden's accommodations, and had a king-sized bed and a private bath with Jacuzzi, as well as fine furnishings handpicked by the prisoner.

For company, Escobar had six of his top lieutenants, including his brother Roberto. The police were not allowed inside the prison, but the press reported comings and goings from the Cathedral at all hours of the day and night. It soon became evident that Escobar was still running his empire from within the prison walls. Yet, the government did nothing. As the truth about the Cathedral leaked out, Gaviria's popularity plummeted and his strategy for getting the drug lords to surrender became a national joke.

In the following months, mutilated corpses, including those of some of Escobar's most trusted lieutenants, began turning up in the vicinity of the Cathedral. According to rumors, the victims had been kidnapped and taken to the prison, where, under Escobar's supervision, they were tortured and killed.

The brazen killings showed that, even while incarcerated, the drug lord had lost none of his arrogant swagger. The king felt that Colombia's drug trafficking industry owed him big time. After all, he was the one who had stuck his neck out against the state in the fight against extradition, and his terror campaign had benefited all of the country's traffickers. He began referring to his war against the Colombian state as "my struggle" and demanded that his associates in the Medellin cartel pay him "taxes" – as a fee for every shipment they made.

"The problem with Escobar is that he began to kidnap all the people closest to him," Gabriel Toboada, a U.S. prisoner and former Medellin cartel member, told the U.S. Senate Subcommittee on Terrorism, Narcotics and International Operations in 1994. "He became a person who wanted to do evil to everybody. From his compadres he knew how much each politician had earned, how much each member of the Medellin cartel had earned, and he began to demand money from them, because he said that he was the one who put his name forward in the fight against extradition, and this thing went out of control."

Giraldo and William Julio Moncada and Fernando and Mario Galeano were among the Escobar associates who refused to pay. They, too, were lured to the Cathedral and, in July 1992, authorities found their mutilated corpses on a roadside a few miles from the prison. After the press reported the killings, the Gaviria administration launched an investigation to find out what was going on at the Cathedral.

To no one's surprise, the government reported what every Colombian knew – Escobar was actually running the place. He had to be moved to a high-security prison, Gaviria decided, but Escobar learned of the government's plans while watching the evening news on television. It was time to check out.

In July 1993, Escobar sneaked away into the night, even though 500 soldiers surrounded the prison. He first fled to a ranch, La Romelia, and waited in a hiding place until the initial search patrols left the area and the commotion surrounding his escape subsided. Then Escobar moved to Llanogrande, close to Rionegro, and renewed his life as a fugitive. Once again, the Patron had embarrassed the state. Gaviria knew he had to recapture the drug lord or forget about having an honorable place in Colombian history.

This time Escobar would have a much more difficult time eluding his enemies, for Search Block was just one foe among exit the king many he had to worry about. The families of the Moncadas and Galeanos had vowed revenge and were scheming to exact it. The associates who still remained alive were tired of his bullying ways and of having to put up money to finance his wars with the state. They did not want to be next to be lured to a meeting with El Patron, only to be summarily tortured and killed.

Even his powerful paramilitary allies began to wonder if they could trust Pablo. Paramilitary leader Fidel Castano, who was good friends with the Galeanos and the Moncadas as well an associate of Escobar, was on the "guest" list at the Cathedral the night they were killed. So Escobar had few allies upon whom he could count for strong support. And he also had to worry about the godfathers in Cali, who knew they would never have a good night's sleep until they removed their bitter enemy from the scene.

On 30 January 1993, a bomb exploded in downtown Bogota, killing twenty people. It was narco war as usual in Colombia. The country's public enemy number one had sent a message to the nation: *Brace yourself. I'm back in the business of attacking the state and unleashing mayhem.* But then there was a surprise. The following day, two bombs – one containing an estimated 100 kilos of dynamite and the other containing eighty kilos – exploded in Medellin in front of apartment buildings where Escobar's wife, two children, his sister and his mother-in-law were staying. It was another close call for the Boss.

Meanwhile, five men showed up at the weekend country retreat of Escobar's mother, located about forty-five miles from Medellin, ordered the lone caretaker out and blew up the place. In a communiqué released to the press on February 2, a new group calling itself "Persecuted by Pablo Escobar" (*Los Pepes*) claimed responsibility for the attacks. The communiqué declared that *Pepes* were working toward "the total elimination of Pablo Escobar, his followers, and his assets to give him a taste of his medicine, which he unfairly dishes out to so many."

Escobar struck back. Mid-morning on February 15th, two powerful bombs exploded five minutes and twelve blocks apart in downtown Bogota, killing four people and injuring more than 100 others. They were the fifth and sixth car bombs since Escobar's mid-January declaration of war against the state. But a few hours later, in Medellin, unidentified men traveling in a blue Toyota camper torched an Escobar-owned luxury house in the exclusive El Poblado section.

It was the *Pepes* again, showing they meant what they had vowed – tit for tat each time Escobar committed a terrorist act. Two days later, gunmen killed Carlos Mario Ossa, a high ranking Escobar financier who was helping to pay for Escobar's terrorist campaign. The same day, Carlos Alzate, a coordinator of Escobar's *sicario* groups, surrendered. Ossa was a key person in passing instructions from Escobar to Alzate, and with Ossa's death, Alzate had no way of communicating with the Patron. Better to come out of the cold than to end up in a morgue. The *Pepes* were seriously starting to disrupt Escobar's organization.

But on March 5<sup>th</sup>, the *Pepes* declared a ceasefire, giving no reason for their action, although the press speculated that it was done to give Escobar time to surrender. That did not happen, and exactly one month later the *Pepes* issued another communiqué, announcing their "commitment to the total annihilation of Escobar," even if "he was captured and put in jail." In other words, the *Pepes* were saying, "We will get you, Pablo, no matter what you do."

The *Pepes* continued to attack Escobar's infrastructure, causing anyone associated with him to fear for their lives. Assassins gunned down two lawyers employed by Escobar's brother Roberto and associate Carlos Alzate. The same day, the *Pepes* killed Escobar's most important attorney, Guido Parra, and Parra's eighteen-year-old son in retaliation for Escobar's north Bogota car bomb that killed eleven and injured over 200 people.

It became obvious that the *Pepes* were actually trying not only to kill Escobar but also to humiliate him. That was evident when they stole "Terremoto," a stallion owned by exit the king Escobar's brother Roberto and valued at more than $1 million, and then returned it in a slightly altered condition – gelded. Terremoto was tied to a sign that read: "We return the horse to the terrible Escobar and his brother." The *Pepes* also murdered Roberto's horse trainer, Oscar

Cardona Zuleta. In a cable, the U.S. embassy noted, "The loss of Terremoto as a sire is seen locally as a grave insult to the Escobars."

The carnage caused by the *Pepes* was unremitting. By mid-November, they had assassinated fifty of Escobar's people, including his brother-in-law, and destroyed some twenty properties belonging to his relatives and associates. The vigilantes could not catch the big fish, but they were slowly poisoning the sea in which it swam. They were embarrassing the Colombian government as well. Why was not the Gaviria administration getting control of the situation, Colombians wondered? Are the *Pepes* and government working together?

Gustavo De Greiff, the country's prosecuting attorney general, said that his office seriously tried to investigate the *Pepes*, but it was never able to get any good information or leads on the people behind it. When the Gaviria administration issued a $1.39-million dollar reward for the capture of the *Pepes'* leaders, the group once again announced its intention to disband. Escobar, however, was not impressed. The drug lord suspected the government and the *Pepes* were in cahoots against him, and he didn't believe the administration had any real intentions of identifying the people behind *Los Pepes*.

In a letter to the government dated August 29th, Escobar charged that "the government offers rewards for the leaders of the Medellin Cartel and for the leaders of the guerrillas, but it doesn't offer rewards for the leaders of the paramilitaries, nor for those of the Cali Cartel, authors of various car bombs in the city of Medellin." He identified the individuals whom he believed to be behind the *Pepes*: the four leaders of the Cali cartel (the Rodriguez brothers, Santacruz Londono, and Herrera) and paramilitary leader Carlos Castano.

Were the *Pepes* and the Colombian government working together? During the period that the *Pepes* launched their campaign against Escobar, U.S. and Colombian officials publicly denied the Cali cartel had supplied them with information that was helping in the hunt for Escobar. Today, officials readily acknowledge that the men from Cali played the key role in taking down Escobar. "As soon as Escobar killed the Galeanos and Moncadas, their people saw themselves as vulnerable and they ran to the Cali cartel and said, '*We want to change sides*,'" said Joe Toft, chief of the DEA's Bogota office from 1988 to 1994. "The Cali people said, 'Okay, if you want to change sides, you need to pay us.' A lot of money changed hands."

The Colombian government was in a death struggle with Escobar and it did not care where information came from, so long as it was credible. "The Colombian government wasn't going to get information about Escobar from the Vatican," explained Robert Nieves, the DEA's chief of international operations from 1989 to 1995. "Sometimes, having to deal with scumbags is the nature of the beast.

Sometimes, you have to get into the sewer because that's where you'll get the best information."

The Cali intelligence operation rivaled those of many governments and this was a major factor in taking down Escobar, sources confirmed. As Ernesto Samper, Colombia's former president, explained, "The cartel's intelligence network was the *key element*." The Cali mafia had a highly sophisticated computer system that they used to gather information on the Medellín cartel, which helps to explain why the *Pepes* were able to find and kill so many rivals when they were most vulnerable.

The cartel kept its computer system in Bogota before moving it to Cali. Always in step with state-of-the-art technology, the cartel replaced it with a more sophisticated and expensive system that Santacruz bought in the United States and kept in one of his businesses. Still, some former U.S. officials remained ambivalent about the cartel's assistance. "No question the [Colombian] government was getting intelligence about Escobar from the Cali cartel," said Robert Gelbard, who served as assistant secretary of state for Latin American affairs during the hunt for Escobar. "In some ways that was all right, but it wasn't all right that the Cali cartel bought off some members of the Colombian government."

In September 1995, an interview with Pacho Herrera appeared in *El Tiempo*. The reporter asked him, "How did you bring down Pablo Escobar?" Herrera replied, "I spent a fortune on that. I paid informants so that they would pass information to the law, and the law annihilated Pablo Escobar. Personally or physically, I never contributed anything." Herrera denied ever being involved with the *Pepes*, but after the *Pepes* episode, reports were published alleging that the United States had turned a blind eye to the ruthless actions of Herrera and his associates.

In an article in the *Miami Herald*, Colonel Oscar Naranjo, the director of the Colombian police intelligence services during the search for Escobar, said that American drug agencies knew of the direct channel of communications existing between the police and the *Pepes* and that American anti-drug agencies knew of its existence and took advantage of it." A source known as "Ruben," who had been a *Pepes* member, asserted that the group had actually kept in contact with DEA agent Javier Pena, who worked in Medellin as the DEA's liaison to Search Block. *Time* magazine also reported that Carlos Castano visited Disneyland as a reward for his work in getting Escobar, which Amnesty International characterized as a euphemism for his work for the *Pepes*.

In his autobiography, *My Confession*, published in 2001, paramilitary leader Carlos Castano said he met with Gilberto Rodriguez seven times and loaned him helicopters. "They were the bosses," recalled Castano in reference to the Cali godfathers. "It's normal to have these types of relations in a country like Colombia."

Paul Paz y Minao, a spokesperson for Amnesty International, said that revelations about the U.S. connection to the *Pepes* raised the question as to whether the U.S. government acted within the law. "The organization was illegal and it committed criminal acts," he explained. "U.S. law forbids government agencies from collaborating with them." Amnesty International filed lawsuits to get access to CIA records relating to the *Pepes*.

Both the Cali cartel and U.S. government intelligence helped get Escobar, along with input from the elite Delta Force unit of American Special Forces troops, but U.S. officials stressed that good police work done by Colombian security forces on the case should not be underestimated. "I know Delta Force is credited with being the difference, but we shouldn't give it too much credit," Pena explained. "To do so is to short-change the Colombian National Police. The Delta Force is good at what they do and they did train the Colombian police how to read coordinates and plan the operations, but Delta Force was never directly involved, lthough they did provide logistical support."

As the *Pepes* and the Colombian government destroyed Escobar's infrastructure, he became desperate for his family's safety and tried to get his wife, Maria Victoria Henao, and their children out of Colombia. Colombian immigration authorities, however, denied his wife permission because she didn't have Pablo's written approval. Morris Busby, U.S. ambassador to Colombia, noted in a cable that

Escobar's "continued efforts to get his children out of Colombia and to re-constitute his terrorist bombs suggest that he has not given up on his war against the government, but consistent police work that target his trafficking and terrorist infrastructure are threatening his plans."

Colombia's nightmare ended on 2 December 1993, when the alliance of the CNP, U.S. law enforcement and the *Pepes* achieved their objective of poisoning the sea around the big fish. When all the escapes and violence had ended, Escobar was alone with a single bodyguard, Alvaro de Jesus Aguela, in a middle-class, two-story house in a Medellin barrio. Using the high-tech equipment supplied by the United States, Search Block intercepted a call Escobar made to his family, who were holed up in room 2908 of the Residencia Tequendama in Bogota. Security personnel surrounded the house and cut the telephone lines in the barrio so no one could warn the drug lord.

Escobar never had a chance. Authorities knocked the door down and stormed the apartment. Dressed only in a T-shirt and jeans, Escobar tried to flee to the roof, but his pursuers gunned him down. Autopsy reports later showed that he had been hit three times, with a shot to the head killing him instantly.

Escobar's death raised a relevant question. Had he been killed trying to flee or was he executed? Most Colombians could care less. A Bogota radio station reported the news of Escobar's death in mantra like fashion, while in the background, carolers sang "Joy to the World." Colombian newspapers, once bludgeoned into timidity by Escobar's power and violence, printed in bold headlines, "Escobar has fallen!" "The King is dead!" When Cali radio stations broadcast the good news, residents celebrated by forming caravans of horn tooting automobiles and waving white flags from the Rodriguez-owned Drogas La Rebaja pharmacies.

An elated Cesar Gaviria called Ambassador Busby to thank him for all the assistance the U.S. gave Colombia in its hunt for Pablo, and Busby, in turn, called Colombia's defense and foreign ministries to congratulate them. The U.S. embassy in Bogota issued a press release congratulating the Colombian government.

A spy in the CNP called Miguel Rodriguez from Medellin to inform him of the good news. Miguel immediately called his brother Gilberto, and during the conversation, he began to cry. Later he hugged his startled accountant Guillermo Pallomari. The uncharacteristic gesture from the normally intense and business-like Godfather frightened the accountant and revealed how much strain the gentlemen from Cali were under in their war with Escobar. According to Pallomari, Miguel then got on his private line and called Gustavo De Greiff to inform him.

On December 18th, less than ten days after being put in isolation in Itagui Prison in Medellin to protect him from his enemies, Pablo's brother Roberto received a package. As he tried to open it, it exploded in his face. The package had the seal of the prosecuting general's office, and prison officials had not opened it because they believed it carried privileged information. The package should have been x-rayed as part of normal security procedures, but the equipment curiously malfunctioned about an hour before the package arrived.

Roberto suffered severe damage to both eyes, and he was transferred to a hospital for surgery. Colombian authorities launched an investigation the day after to see if the three guards who handled the letter had any link to the perpetrators. In a report to the State Department, the U.S. embassy in Bogota assessed, "while no one has yet claimed responsibility for the attack on Roberto Escobar, the *Pepes* are the most likely suspects." Escobar's family remained in seclusion at the Tequendama Hotel in Bogota, still looking for a country to accept them.

Pablo's eight-year-old daughter Manuela made an emotional appeal on television to the *Pepes*, imploring them to stop their attacks on her family, and another one to President Gaviria, asking him to help them leave the country. "What have I done for this to be happening to me?" Manuela asked.

Cali's godfathers felt relieved that their bitter enemy was finally buried in a grave, but they were uncomfortable with being crowned "the New Kings of Cocaine" by the press. What course of action the Colombian and U.S. governments would take in the War on Drugs remained uncertain. Some U.S. officials, such as Robert C. Bryden, the head of the DEA's New York regional office, pointed out that the Cali cartel now had no competition, "so they can go on any corner of any city in this country [the U.S.] and nobody in the drug business can oppose them."

Other analysts and law enforcement officials wondered how aggressively the Colombian government would pursue a more peaceful breed of drug trafficker not known for narco-terrorism. Still, the Colombian government announced it would keep Search Block together to begin their pursuit of the Cali cartel.

In its hunt for Escobar, the U.S. and Colombian governments had not totally ignored Cali. Even as the pursuit of Escobar intensified, authorities were working to penetrate Cali's infrastructure. They conducted a series of raids on drug processing labs, official residences, and office residences belonging to the godfathers, destroying nearly twenty tons of processed cocaine and 100 laboratories.

In January 1992, the Colombian security forces conducted their first operation against the cartel's money-laundering operations, carrying out thirty-two simultaneous raids, not only in Cali but also in Bogota and Baranquilla. They seized numerous computers, floppy disks and 20,000 other financial records and uncovered information that led to three arrests and the freezing of $15 million in bank accounts in Colombia, Britain, Germany, Hong Kong, and the United States.

By March 1992, U.S. officials began to see a change in the cartel. In a cable, the U.S. embassy noted, "The Cali cartel is very concerned about the capabilities of the U.S. government to interfere with their operations. They appear to be paranoid." As evidence of their paranoia, the report noted that the godfathers were living less ostentatiously and driving cars built and sold in Colombia as an effort to keep a low profile in an environment that was increasingly hostile to them.

Through Operation Belalcazar III, authorities arrested Diego Martin Buitrago on September 18, 1993, one of the cartel's major contacts in Cali. On December 1st, police raided an estate near Cali belonging to Jose Santacruz Londono. Ambassador Busby told his superiors in Washington D.C. that "Pablo Escobar's death and the disabling of the Medellin cartel are great successes for Colombia, but now they should continue with the Cali cartel."

On December 13th, the U.S. embassy announced that 120 U.S. army engineers were arriving in Colombia in late December to undertake a ten-week construction project in the jungle village of Juanchaco, about seventy-five miles from Cali. Officials from both countries insisted that the troops were there solely to build schools and roads, but many Cali residents believed the project's true purpose was to construct a major base to gather intelligence and stage raids on the cartel infrastructure.

In late December, the press reported that lawyers for the

Cali cartel and officials from the office of Prosecuting Attorney General Gustavo De Greiff's office had made contact and were negotiating. A special jail was being built to accommodate up to 300 gang members, including three of the godfathers, who were planning to surrender, or so the story went. Under an agreement, said the rumor mill, the godfathers would keep their assets and get light sentences, as little as two years.

Meanwhile the cartel was exploring its options in the post-Escobar period. Its leaders held an important meeting to discuss their future and how they could increase drug trafficking to the United States and grow internationally. "We need to control the drug trafficking market at the world level," Miguel told his partners. "We need to be able to set the price and to control the price." The cartel had big dreams and big plans, but its next nightmare was already taking shape.

# CHAPTER EIGHT

# TAKEDOWN

**T**HE SHOWDOWN BETWEEN the Cali Cartel and Pablo Escobar had been inevitable. The War of the Cartels was the result. No exact statistics for the number killed in the ensuing vicious war of attrition are available, but thousands of gangsters, as well as judges, police, lawyers, journalists and Colombian man-in-the-street, were murdered. When the War of the Cartels ended on December 2, 1993, Escobar lay dead on a Medellin rooftop, and the brothers Rodriguez Orejuela stood alone as the undisputed Kings of Cocaine.

But being crowned number one in the illegal drug world was not the position in which the Cali Cartel should have been. Indeed, that lofty status, lead to its eventual downfall. The US had begun specifically targeting the Cali mob in 1991 after discovering 12,500 kilos of the Rodriguez brothers' cocaine hidden in concrete posts on a ship in Miami. This sparked the Operation Cornerstone investigation, and in the ensuing years, the U.S. authorities would go on to seize 50,000 kilos of cocaine and apprehend nearly 100 Cali operatives in the US. The intelligence that Uncle Sam gathered was used to piece together knowledge of the cartel's empire, and when Escobar finally left the picture, taking down the Cali mob became law enforcement's prime goal.

A massive break came on May 18, 1994, when Colombian authorities confiscated an IBM AS/400 computer worth a cool million dollars from a high-ranking associate of the brothers Rodriguez. To this date, the super computer is the most sophisticated piece of technology ever taken from drug traffickers. It took the DEA several months before its computer experts could break into it.

What the DEA found was mind boggling—computer files containing information on thousands of bribes the cartel paid to Colombians from all sectors of society, as well as Colombia's entire motor vehicle records. "If you were a Colombian and wanted a U.S. visa, you might call the U.S. Embassy in Bogota once or perhaps twice for information," explains Steve Casto, a DEA intelligence agent who analyzed the cartel's super computer. "But what if you were an informant and calling once or twice a month? The Cali cartel would find this pattern by analyzing the telephone records. Then the cartel would wire tap the calls that person was making to the U.S. Embassy."

By 1995, the Colombian government assigned 500 soldiers and police to a unit known as Search Block to track and take down the Rodriguez brothers and their key subordinates. The authorities conducted a series of raids and dropped hundreds of leaflets on Cali announcing a reward of $1.6 million for information leading to the capture of Gilberto and Miguel.

But nothing happened. Search Block would show up at a house, apartment or business, only to learn that one of the brothers had just fled. Corruption was still rampant and the government had to fire 174 police officers, including 48 captains and other high ranking officers, with ties to the Cali cartel.

The Colombian authorities, with the help of the U.S. authorities, doggedly pursued the investigation. Most the cartel's operatives were deathly afraid of snitching against the powerful cartel, but eventually a couple of their associates did and this proved to be another big break for the authorities.

The first to turn was Harold Ackerman, who was such an important cell head that he was known as "the Cali cartel's ambassador to the United States." He was the prototypical Cali manager and the type of employee who helped make the cartel the world's most powerful and successful criminal multinational.

Born in Palmira, Colombia, in 1941, Ackerman graduated from a university in Cali where he studied industrial engineering and business administration before joining a clothing manufacturing business. He came to the United States in June 1981 and opened a dress shop in the Dadeland Mall. "I was living well, but one day some Colombians started coming by my shop and hanging out," Ackerman recalled. "They kept telling me that I could make a lot more money working for an organization based in Cali."

Soon after joining the Cali cartel, the money began to roll in for Ackerman. In October 1991, Ackerman earned his first $120,000 by helping to smuggle to the United States a 5,000-kilo cocaine shipment concealed in frozen broccoli. Two months later there was a second shipment, an importation by Southeast Agrotrade into the port of Everglades, Florida, of 5,000 kilograms of cocaine, once again hidden in frozen broccoli; this second shipment earned him another $200,000. Ackerman earned another $400,000 for a third shipment of 2,000 kilos of cocaine in early February, using the same route as the first one. Ackerman estimates that he earned $3 million during the two years he worked for the organization.

On April 23rd, federal investigators raided Harold Ackerman's luxurious home in North Miami. They were amazed at what they found – $462,000 in cash in a safe, $200,000 worth of jewelry, and a Lexus, a Toyota Tercel, a Mazda RX-7 and two BMWs, all uncovered after a search of the property. "It was obvious that he liked the good life and needed a lot of money to keep up his lifestyle," said

Lee Granato, a U.S. customs agent who investigated the financial aspect of Operation Cornerstone. Keeping his mouth shut and not cooperating with the U.S. government, if the authorities arrested him, was one rule Ackerman knew he could not break. He had too many family members in Colombia, vulnerable to retaliation. Just in case, Miguel used William Moran, one of his lawyers, to relay messages to Ackerman. Some were reassuring. "Don't be concerned, Harold. Take it easy. Your family will receive a monthly payment."

But Moran also relayed this message, "Mr. Rodriguez told me to remind you that as a friend, he is a very good person, but as an enemy, he will be a very bad person. Think of cooperating and not even your dog will remain. Remember, you still have family in Colombia."

Harold Ackerman has a simple and direct answer when asked to explain why he changed his mind and decided to cooperate with U.S. prosecutors. "Six life sentences," he said with a laugh. After some reflection, he elaborated, "I also had to take care of my family, and I couldn't do that spending the rest of my life behind bars. I agreed to testify because the prosecutors said they could protect my family if I testified, and I believed them."

Ackerman became one of the most important witnesses ever to testify against the Cali cartel and his testimony helped make Operation Cornerstone one of the most significant criminal investigations in U.S. history. "Most flips are either sneaky or stupid or both," Ryan explained. "But in interrogating Harold, it was like talking to a sharp businessman. We never caught him in a lie. He probably spent three weeks on the witness stand over the course of two trials. He was the most important witness I ever worked with and the best as well." In noting his personal contribution to the Cornerstone investigation, Ackerman later testified, "My cooperation with the United States provided a detailed, minute and true narration of my activities in narcotics smuggling. I was involved with the Rodriguez Orejuela organization."

This cooperation also included the explanation of the organization's flow chart, the structure of the Cali organization, its operation methods, as well as providing the positive identification of other persons involved in the organization, the identification of other routes of importation and distribution of cocaine in the United States, and a precise and exact analysis of the participation and the activities of the U.S. attorneys who worked on behalf of the cartel. And as a result of this information, a number of investigations and operations were begun against the Cali cartel.

Micromanager, always-in-control Miguel Rodriguez had a hard time handling the news of Ackerman's defection. "It was a very stunning piece of news, quite serious, and it made him physically ill," Pallomari recalled. Miguel and the other godfathers held more crisis management meetings to discuss the state of their empire. All their big plans to dominate the world's illegal drug market were unraveling. They needed lots of money to keep their giant criminal multinational organization afloat, but the arrest of Ackerman and the other associates, who seemed to be falling like dominos, was drying up the pool of managers and the flow of money and disrupting distribution.

The second important Cali Cartel associate to turn was Guillermo Pallomari, the Cali cartel's chief accountant. By the summer of 1995, Pallomari had become the *Man Who Knew Too Much*, for he had sat in on most of the cartel's important meetings and kept track of hundreds of legal and illegal documents. In April 1995, the Colombian government accused him of the crime of serving as a front man for a criminal enterprise and called him in for questioning.

Miguel Rodriguez thought Pallomari was going to crack and knew time was short. If police caught Pallomari, he would be a devastating witness against him. Miguel put a contract out on his former accountant's life, but Pallomari had time to go underground in Cali. Pallomari realized his only chance to stay alive was to turn himself in. So he called the U.S. embassy in Bogota to make arrangements. His wife Patricia Cardona agreed to join him, but first she needed to take care of some business matters. DEA's agents visited Cardona and urged her to turn herself in to the U.S. embassy. "We have intelligence that your life is in danger," they told her.

In August, Pallomari arrived in Bogota at the U.S. embassy and met with the DEA to arrange details about his surrender and cooperation. In return for his testimony, Pallomari would join the witness protection program. The day after the DEA agents visited Cardona, Pallomari tried calling her at their home, her office, and her family's residence. She was nowhere to be found, Pallomari never saw his wife again.

On 16 August 1995, Cardona and Freddie Vivas Yangus, her employee, vanished without a trace. They were never seen again, although there is a record that Cardona left Colombia and traveled to Lima, Peru. A few days later, Pallomari and his two sons made their way to an undisclosed location in the United States via a commercial airline with the DEA's assistance. He was brought before a judge in Miami, and on 15 December 1998, he pleaded guilty to racketeering conspiracy and money laundering charges. He cooperated with U.S. authorities and was placed in the Federal Witness Protection Program. One senior administration official told the Washington Post, "he may turn out to be the biggest witness of international drug trafficking that we've ever had."

By now, the Cali Cartel had lost its corrupt grip on the Colombian political system when the narco cassette scandal erupted and became Colombia; version of Watergate. On June 15, 1994, during the 1994 Colombia presidential elections, presidential candidate Andres Pastrana was on a campaign swing through Cali when an unidentified man

handed him several cassette tapes containing some extraordinary conversations obtained from wire intercepts. The
tapes provided irrefutable proof to Pastrana that the Cali
cartel was financing the campaign of his opponent, Ernesto
Samper, to the tune of more than $6 million. .

The cassettes, however, did not have an impact on
the election and Ernesto Samper won in a close vote.
Revelations that his election campaign may have taken
millions of dollars from the Cali cartel, however, forced
Samper into a position of having something to prove. As
Colombian expert Randall Crandall explained, "Knowing that critics in both Colombia and Washington were
highly dubious about Samper's willingness to fight the
War on Drugs, Samper was forced to go further than he
or the United States had ever imagined. Thus we have
the paradoxical situation whereby this supposedly narco
compromised president ended up, whether he liked it or
not, being a reliable and predictable ally with Washington vis-à-vis the drug war."

As a prime suspect involved in shady dealings with drug
kingpins, Samper was in no position to defy the Clinton
administration when it began putting pressure on him to
get more aggressive against the Cali Cartel. Samper had no
choice but to get tough, not just in word but in action.

The Colombian government set up a special command
at the Military Bloque base on the outskirts of Cali, which
included elements of the Colombian police, the army, and

the Search Block. The DEA was given a house on the base, and it began to send agents to Cali to do intelligence work.

The Colombian press was reporting that more than 500 DEA agents were in Cali trying to develop intelligence that could lead them to the capture of the Big Four godfathers (the Rodriguez brothers, Jose Santacruz and Pacho Herrera), but there were never more than two or three agents in the city at any one time. The DEA essentially assigned four agents to help the Colombian authorities track the Rodriguez brothers, who were the two top targets on the hit list.

The continuous pressure and the raids began to have some effect on the cartel's communications network and its cash flow. With rewards of as much as $1.9 million for Miguel and Gilberto Rodriguez and $625,000 for Santacruz and Herrera, the godfathers had to constantly worry about informants and betrayal. The authorities applied pressure by dropping hundreds of "wanted" leaflets on Cali. The supposedly kinder, gentler cartel was not going to take any chances and have somebody rat them out. In one six-week period, about seventy-five dead bodies, some showing signs of torture, turned up in the city.

The DEA began hearing from its CIs (Confidential Informants) about an assistant to Gilberto nicknamed Flaco ("Skinny"). His real name was Alberto Madrid Mayor and he worked as Gilberto's accountant and personal secretary. About thirty-five years old and 5'8" tall, Madrid was known as an impeccable dresser. He had worked for Gilberto since the mid-1990s. "Find and follow Flaco," the informants were telling the DEA, "and he will lead you to Gilberto."

The DEA managed to locate Flaco and put surveillance on him. For the next month, a team of seven to ten CNP members and DEA agents began tailing Flaco, hoping he would lead them to Gilberto Rodriguez. Eventually, they tracked Flacco to a neighborhood and group of townhouses. On June 9, 1995, Gilberto was found hiding in an upscale apartment in Cali. As the authorities made the arrest, the terrified Gilberto exclaimed, "Don't shoot. I'm a man of peace."

The police did not shoot the Chess Player. Still, in arresting Gilberto Rodriguez, Colombia and the United States garnered their first major victory against the Cali cartel. Colombian General Joe Rosso Serrano, who was heading the campaign against the Cali cartel, went to the townhouse to see the prize catch and escorted him on a flight to police headquarters in Bogota. Colombian television showed footage of the helicopter landing and heavily armed police hustling an unshaven and handcuffed prisoner out of the airport. It was a festive occasion at the CNP headquarters when Gilberto's escort arrived. Workers cheered as if they were at a soccer game and threw confetti on law officers who gathered to announce the arrest.

The Colombian government was ecstatic. "For the first time, the world could clearly see that we were serious about defeating the Cali cartel," said President Ernesto Samper.

"This arrest sent a signal to the other narco traffickers that their insidious crimes would not be allowed to destroy the fabric of our people." Based on interviews with Clinton administration officials, the *New York Times* reported that "the capture of the most influential leader of the world's largest drug trafficking gang in Colombia. . . was the best news United States officials had gotten in years in the long running battle against drugs."

Rodriguez faced up to twenty-four years in prison on drug trafficking and illegal enrichment charges, and there were several indictments against him in various U.S. cities. Still, if his stable of high-powered lawyers could gain for him the full benefits available under the Colombian penal code, he would have to spend no more than five years in jail. At this time, the Chess Player's extradition to the United States was not even a remote possibility, since the authorities had no evidence that he committed any crimes after 17 December 1997, the date the latest extradition law went into effect.

In captivity, Gilberto continued to play his innocence charade, rejecting the charges against him and denying he ever led the Cali cartel, which he said was an invention of the DEA. The day after his arrest, a bomb ripped through a street festival in the Parque San Antonio in downtown Medellin, killing twenty-one and wounding more than 200 people.

Anonymous telephone callers, claiming to be drug traffickers, said they carried out the bombing in reprisal for Rodriguez's arrest. The bomb was a chilling flashback to the worst terrorism of the Escobar era, and an anxious public wondered if it was déjà vu. No terrorist bombing, however, was going to distract the Colombian authorities, who were fired up by their sudden victory over Escobar and the Medellin cartel and now focused on Miguel Rodriguez, the real Señor, or boss.

The DEA contacted Jorge Salcedo to see if he would be interested in defecting. They met to discuss the details of their arrangement. "The DEA appreciates your help," the agents told Salcedo, "and you will be nicely rewarded. Be assured that we will get you and your family out of Colombia." Their first meeting went well and they agreed to get together again the next evening at 5 P.M. "I will try to dig out more information about Miguel's exact whereabouts," Salcedo reassured the DEA agents.

The agents met with "Sean," the codename they now used to identify their CI, several times over the next two days, and Salcedo continued to provide valuable information. He said that Miguel was hiding in apartment 402 or 801 at 3rd West Avenue, Number 13–86, in a barrio known as Santa Rita. At 5:30 p.m. on July 15, 1995, a team of Colombian police officers and DEA and CIA agents moved to the target in two-rented chicken trucks. Miguel, however, had time to flee behind the apartment wall into his specially built hiding place know as a *caleta*. Just as the DEA agents on the scene figured out where Miguel was most likely hiding, a Colombian government official arrived and ordered them to leave, accusing them of operating illegally in Colombia. The charge was bogus and the DEA agents were allowed to return later to the apartment, but Miguel, with the help of corrupt cops, was long gone.

The brothers suspected a mole and Salcedo was now in great danger. Still, he provided the DEA with more information on Miguel's new hiding place. On July 21, Feistl and Mitchell talked with Sean on the telephone. The CI had a good lead to Miguel's new hideout. Three days later they talked again and Sean told them he was sending the agents a package containing a map and a photo of the apartment where he thought Miguel was hiding now: Hacienda Buenas Aires, West Street, Number 5A-50. The new location looked a lot more upscale than apartment 402.

Each floor contained one apartment of about 3,000 to 4,000 square feet, certainly a lot more area to cover in searching for Miguel's *caleta*. The next day a DEA employee went to the airport to pick up the package. On August 1st, DEA agents traveled to Cali to begin the surveillance of Hacienda Buenas Aires. The agents knew Miguel was a night owl who liked to stay up until the early hours of the morning, so they began the surveillance about ten at night. They figured there would be a good chance that the last light to go out in the building would identify the apartment in which Miguel was hiding. Sean said the two black maids were definitely with Miguel this time. Hopefully they would spot them.

During the next four days, the agents conducted surveillance of the apartment. The assignment actually turned out to be fun. The square was a hangout for the locals, a place where they could buy beer and candy. The agents sipped on beers and watched the burning cane fields in the distance. No one could tell that they were actually spying on the tall building in front of them. The last apartment's lights to go off were on the tenth floor, but they could not see anybody in it. Then on August 4th, when the agents were about to call it a night, the lights in the tenth-floor apartment came on again at 2 A.M. There they were! Feistl spotted the two black maids doing something in the kitchen, cooking and washing dishes. The authorities could now make their move.

Colombian and U.S. officials huddled and decided the raid would happen on August 6th. The success of the operation would depend on the element of surprise – getting into the apartment before Miguel could get into one of those amazing *caletas*. There were two avenues of approach to the apartment: the road in front of it and a canal or drainage ditch behind it. To get to the canal, the search team had to climb a steep hill of about 100 yards. The plan was for the navy team to go and down the hill, run through the drainage ditch, and surprise and neutralize the security guards so they could not sound the alarm.

The DEA rented a dump truck that could carry in the back the police personnel conducting the search. There was a great deal of construction in the area at the time and a dump truck would not arouse suspicion. To coordinate the raid, the two units communicated by cellphone. This time, the operation moved like clockwork. At four in the morning, the two attack teams converged on the front door of Miguel's apartment. The DEA had made sure the search team had legal permission from prosecuting attorney general Alfonso Valdivieso to knock the door down, so there would be no delay or problems in quickly entering the apartment. A navy sailor battered the door down with a sledgehammer. Once inside, the team immediately spotted Jesus "Mateo" Zapata, Miguel's personal secretary and driver; Miguel's first wife, Ampara Arbalaez; and two black maids – but no Miguel.

The team raced through the apartment. It was beautiful and much bigger than 402. Nice marble floors, a pool table, an exercise bike. There were numerous phone lines coming in, the sure sign it was a safe house. And then a young navy officer spotted Miguel trying to climb into his *caleta*, a five-door file cabinet built into the wall. He grabbed Miguel. "I got him! I got him!" he yelled.

Miguel was in his boxer shorts, barely awake. He had tried to scurry to his hiding place, which had all the comforts of home: snacks, bottled water, an oxygen tank to breathe, a stool, and a copy of Colombia's penal code.

Miguel's reaction was one of total disbelief. "Who found me? How did they do it?" When he spotted the gringos, his attitude changed and he seemed resigned to his fate. He even sat calmly for a trophy photo with the DEA agents and a CNP officer.

Half an hour later, police put Miguel in a jeep and took him to the police base. Miguel's escort was so excited that they went much too fast for his liking. "Slow down!" Miguel barked, acting as if he was still the CEO of a multi-billion-dollar crime multinational. "What's the rush? You already got me."

# CHAPTER NINE

# WITH A WHIMPER

**W**ITH **MIGUEL RODRIGUEZ** Orejuela's capture, six of the top seven leaders of the Cali cartel were now behind bars. The seventh, Chepe Santacruz, was dead. Chepe had escaped from the maximum-security wing of Bogota's La Picota prison with the help of a group of associates posing as interrogators. Prosecutors had visited the prisoner earlier in the morning and left at midday. Another car arrived with the "interrogators" about midday under the ruse of continuing the inquiry, but they whisked Chepe away to freedom. Military and intelligence units combed Cali and Bogota, but they found no leads to his whereabouts. The Colombian government offered a $2 million reward for Chepe's recapture.

What happened next remains uncertain. The official report was that Santacruz was killed in a shootout with police on 5 August 1996. The DEA agents who saw the autopsy photos, however, say Chepe's body showed signs of torture. Santacruz's family called for a second autopsy after its lawyer, veteran Cali cartel house counsel Guillermo Villa, charged that the police "converted deterrent orders into physical execution orders." Serrano defended the forensic examination conducted in Medellin by experts and countered that Villa "should not be exercising his profession with the background he has." Chepe was buried in a Cali cemetery without the second autopsy. Today, many sources still remain skeptical of the official account.

With Santacruz dead, the eighth and only remaining Cali godfather still free was Pacho Herrera. On 1 September 1996, after months of negotiation, Pacho Herrera arrived at Bloque de Busqueda police base in Cali to surrender directly to General Serrano. DEA agent Dave Mitchell was at the base and Serrano allowed him to debrief Pacho after the drug lord asked to see him.

"When Pacho arrived at the base, he looked as if he had just left a *GQ* fashion show," Mitchell recalled. "He wore an expensive suit, a tie, and aviator-style glasses and looked more like a businessman than a drug trafficker facing several indictments in the United States. He was very friendly but evasive in our interview, and didn't really tell me anything."

But Herrera did turn informant, implicating thirty-five people, including some of his own family members, in being cartel members. In return, Herrera received a sentence of six years and eight months and a fine of one million dollars for the crime of drug trafficking.

On 5 November 1998, Pacho was playing a game of football in the maximum security area at the Palmira prison when a well-dressed man, posing as lawyer, strolled up to him, embraced him warmly, and then pulled out a gun and shot him six times in the head. Eight days later, Pacho's paraplegic brother, who was also in prison, fired shots from his electric wheelchair and killed another inmate, Orlando Henao-Montoya, the same drug trafficker who was responsible for Chepe's death and who was believed to be the architect of Pacho's killing.

The cartel was now on life support. Yet, while the government was successfully pursuing the remaining Cali leaders, Miguel and Gilberto lived more like guests than criminals in La Picota prison, thanks to the incorrigibly corrupt Colombian penal system. The brothers used cellphones and a suspected communications network run through a pay phone at the prison to oversee their business interests.

The brothers' families and lawyers came and went as they pleased, carrying their messages to and from the prison. In one week, Gilberto received 123 visits from his lawyers. Their prison cells looked more like upscale apartments and included cable television, expensive stereo sound systems, carpeting, and adjoining private bathrooms. Imagine an incarcerated John Gotti or Carlos Lehder having their meals especially prepared for them in an American prison, but that's the type of cuisine the Rodriguez brothers were able to enjoy. In one search of the prison section in which the Rodriguez brothers were held, police found four bottles of French wine and twelve bottles of Scotch.

Miguel operated a small kiosk, called "Poor Miguel's Shop," which sold shortbread, aspirins, Cote d'Or chocolate from Belgium, and soft drinks over the counter to visitors. For being an entrepreneur within prison walls, Miguel could actually have his sentence reduced by as much as a third.

In January 1997, Gilberto and Miguel were finally convicted for their crimes by a so-called faceless judge. Through plea bargaining by their lawyers, Gilberto received ten-and-a-half years and Miguel, nine years. The sentences were far short of the twenty-four-year maximum that the court could have handed down or the life sentence without parole they would have surely received if they had been extradited to the United States.

Still, it was only the first criminal ruling against the brothers as they still had four more cases pending. The next month, Miguel was sentenced to twenty-three years in jail for a 330-pound cocaine shipment to Tampa in 1989 for which he had refused to accept responsibility. Radio and television reports revealed that the judge in the case was offered a million dollars to let Miguel off the hook. In May 1998, an appeals court judge added five years to the jail sentences of Gilberto and Miguel.

But on November 7, 2002, a Colombian court shook the nation by ordering Gilberto Rodriguez's early release from prison, despite intense pressure from President Alvaro Uribe. Incredibly, the Chess Player had spent less than six years in prison for his crimes. Then four months after releasing the Chess Player from jail, the Colombian government filed new charges against him – his alleged involvement in a 1990 shipment of 330 pounds of cocaine from Colombia to the United States.

Gilberto Rodriguez was back in jail. U.S. officials insisted the Colombian government made the move on its own initiative. The U.S. government continued to investigate the Rodriguez Orejuela brothers with the goal of getting them extradited to the U.S. Indeed, the U.S. government never relented in its aggressive pursuit of Cali cartel money and assets. The Office of Foreign Assets Control (OFAC) in the U.S. Department of the Treasury became the lead agency in the financial investigation of history's richest trafficking organization.

The use of economic sanctions against the cartel's assets would be its punitive tool. The Cali cartel invested the billions of dollars it earned from the drug trade in what looked like legitimate companies, particularly those involved in the production and sale of pharmaceutical drugs, including Laboratorios Kressfor of Colombia and Penta Pharma.

Once the Rodriguez brothers began to be identified in public documents as partners in these companies, they tried to hide their ownership and control as a way of avoiding their seizure by law enforcement authorities. In 1989, Gilberto and Miguel began arranging for their companies to be held under the names of family members and trusted associates. In reality, the brothers Rodriguez owned them and told their associates what to do.

When the Treasury Department announced in December 2000, that it had added the names of eight businesses and eight individuals to its SDNT (Specially Designated Narcotics Trafficker) list, the number of suspected Cali cartel owned blocked had grown to 548. The list included such valuable assets as Copservir and its Drogas de Rebaja drug store chain, the America de Cali professional soccer team (Colombia's equivalent of Manchester United in the United Kingdom), the Cosmepop cosmetics company, the Farmacoop pharmaceutical laboratory, as well as investment, construction, real estate, agricultural and distribution companies.

The biggest humiliation for Gilberto and Miguel came in September 2004 when the Colombian government seized assets of theirs worth $216 million. About 4,000 police, accompanied by more than 450 prosecutors, confiscated for the state 400 Drogas de Rebaja drug stores in twenty-six cities. "This is the most important seizure of assets belonging to the mafia in Colombia's history," said Alfonso Plaza, head of the National Drug Directorate.

OFAC officials agreed. "The death knell for the Cali cartel came when Colombian authorities seized the Drogas de Rebaja drug store chain," said one OFAC official. "The move broke the back of the cartel's financial empire."

The hard work put in by OFAC and its partners in their aggressive attack on the cartel infrastucture was rewarded on March 3, 2004, when R. Richard Newcomb, Director of OFAC, together with David N. Kelley, the U.S. Attorney General for the Southern District of New York, and Anthony Placido, the Special Agent in Charge of the New York Division of the U.S. DEA, announced a two-count indictment and the filing of extradition affidavits requesting that the Colombian government extradite Gilberto and Miguel Rodriguez Orejuela to New York State on money laundering charges. If convicted of all the money laundering and conspiracy charges in the indictment, the brothers faced a maximum sentence of twenty-five years in prison and the forfeiture of $1 billion.

Judgment day for Gilberto Rodriguez arrived on 4 November 2004, when the Colombian Supreme Court ruled that the government could extradite him to the United States for trial. The high court said it was up to the government to decide if it wanted to put the Chess Player on a DEA plane to Miami. That was hardly an agonizing decision for Uribe. On November 9th, he announced he would approve the drug lord's historic extradition.

On 3 December 2004, the Chess Player, who had outwitted authorities for more than thirty years, was taken in an armored vehicle from La Picota maximum security prison in southern Bogota to a military base adjacent to Colombia's international airport. Even now, the authorities were taking no chances. Rodriguez – who was allowed to make one last phone call – wore a bulletproof vest over his brown jacket, as about 120 police officers and soldiers and a convoy of security cars escorted him. A police helicopter hovered overhead. At the airport, Gilberto was handed over to DEA agents representing at about 9:10 pm EST and he was on his way to the United States.

As the Chess Player's criminal career headed towards its sordid conclusion, the remaining question remained was whether brother Miguel would follow him. There was speculation that Colombia would not extradite Miguel because he was on dialysis. U.S. officials were confident, however, though as one explained the day after Gilberto's extradition, "I doubt that the Colombian government will want to skip any legal steps to speed things up. So that everything would be by the book."

In March 2005, President Uribe finally ordered Miguel's extradition, and "El Senor" was flown from Palanquero Air Force to Florida, where the stocky sixty-one-year-old was held without bail. Like his brother, he denied charges of drug trafficking.

January 2006 brought another big breakthrough in the battle to finish off the Cali cartel. William Rodriguez Abadia turned himself in to U.S. agents in Panama in January after years on the run, citing what his lawyer called serious health problems and fears about his security. "It had to be extremely hush, hush, otherwise he wouldn't have made it out of Colombia," Humberto Dominquez, William's Miami-based lawyer, told the press. The balding former drug lord appeared in court clad in blue jeans, a tight blue shirt and ankle chins. He spoke to his lawyer in English and Spanish as Dominquez entered the guilty plea on his behalf.

Then came the real sensation. As his father and uncle languished in the Miami Federal Detention Center, awaiting a September trial, the forty-year-old Abadia agreed to testify against them. He also pleaded guilty to what prosecutors described as his "involvement in a wide-ranging cocaine importation conspiracy that existed from 1990 to July 2002" and was sentenced to nearly 22 years in a federal prison. He admitted helping his father and uncle run their criminal empire from behind prison bars after they were jailed in 1995 and agreed to forfeit his share of a business empire valued at about $300 million.

According to the factual proffer read at his plea hearing, William had been placed in charge of his father's portion of the family business, including Drogas La Rebaja, and helped initiate and manage plans to launder and conceal their drug profits. He was also responsible for arranging bribes and payoffs to incarcerated cartel employees and their families to prevent them from testifying against the brothers. "The guilty plea of William Rodriguez-Abadia is a major victory in the war against drugs," said U.S. Attorney R. Alexander Acosta. "It marks the fall of the Cali cartel. It also sends a signal to all narcotics traffickers that they cannot hide or run from prosecution."

In May 2006, the brothers received a blow to their defense strategy when Magistrate Judge Theodore Klein ruled that federal prosecutors could pursue the brothers for illegal activity dating back to the early 1990s, when the cartel was at the height of its power. The ruling seemed to circumvent the extradition treaty which forbids the extradition of Colombians for crimes committed before 16 December 1997. Judge Klein made clear, however, that the brothers could only be convicted of drug trafficking if the alleged activity occurred both before and after December 16th.

The brothers could see the writing on the wall and that a formidable case had been built against them. Their lawyers began to negotiate. "They knew, no way would they ever get out of a U.S. jail again, and they began to negotiate the best deal they could get for their family," explained one official.

Twenty-eight members of the Rodriguez family, all of whom were on OFAC's Specially Designated List, (SDNT) were brought into the negotiations. They included not only the spouses and children of Miguel and Gilberto, but also their nephews and nieces, all of whom had different levels of involvement in the cartel.

Finally, a deal was hammered out. On September 26th, Gilberto and Miguel, both dressed in dark business suits but shackled at the ankles, appeared before Judge Moreno. The brothers who had almost turned Colombia into a narco democracy appeared humble, mere mortals, who admitted to smuggling conspiracy charges and showed contrition for their life of crime. "I want to apologize to my family and ask for forgiveness for any sufferings I may have caused them," said Miguel softly, through an interpreter. "I'm doing this fully convinced it will bring something better." Gilberto added, "I'm willingly submitting myself to American justice."

The pair pled guilty to conspiracy to smuggle more than 200 kilograms of cocaine into the U.S from Colombia through Central America. They also agreed to plead guilty to charges in the Southern District of New York that they conspired to launder their illicit fortune through their pharmaceutical drug empire, which included more than 400 retail drug stores across Colombia, as well as pharmaceutical companies that manufactured the drugs.

Members of the family also agreed to forfeit their interests and ownership to Rodriguez entities in the U.S. and worldwide. In return, the family members became eligible to be removed from OFAC's black list for crimes committed before 16 December 1997.

The pair pled guilty to conspiracy to smuggle more than 200 kilograms of cocaine into the U.S from Colombia through Central America. They also agreed to plead guilty to charges in the Southern District of New York that they conspired to launder their illicit fortune through their pharmaceutical drug empire, which included more than 400 retail drug stores across Colombia, as well as pharmaceutical companies that manufactured the drugs.

Members of the family also agreed to forfeit their interests and ownership to Rodriguez entities in the U.S. and worldwide. In return, the family members became eligible to be removed from OFAC's black list, so long as they continued to assist the U.S. government in any on-going or related forfeiture actions.

"It is not done deal with the family members," one Treasury Department official explained. "They will have to prove to the U.S. government that they have divested themselves of all properties. Our investigation is still ongoing. The onus is on the family. They will have to make a sincere effort to get rid of all companies and properties."

At a press conference, U.S. officials did their best to portray the outcome of the case as major victory in the War on Drugs. The DEA, U.S. Immigration and Customs Enforcement, the Treasury Department and Justice Department were all represented. "The founding brothers of Colombia's notorious Cali cartel once cornered the world's cocaine market and smuggled it into the U.S. on a colossal scale,'said Karen Tandy, head of the DEA. "Now, after today's conviction, the Cali cartel will be reduced to extinction with its members in American prison like the common criminals they are, stripped of all wealth, power and influence they once possessed."

Immediately following their guilty pleas, Judge Moreno sentenced Gilberto, 67, and Miguel, 62, to eighty-seven months in prison respectively on the money-laundering charges. The sentence would run concurrently with a sentence of thirty years imprisonment Moreno previously imposed as a result of the cocaine trafficking charges in the Southern District of Florida indictment. There was no question that this was judgment day for the Rodriguez brothers. A jail cell in the U.S. would be their tomb.

Still in his forties, William Rodriguez may not have to spend the rest of his in a U.S. tomb. In December 2006, Judge Moreno approved the reduction of William's prior prison sentence by 17 years, from nearly 22 years to 5 years.

Although it is common for judges to cut the sentences of cooperating witnesses, William's sentence reduction caused quite a stir in legal circles. A cut of this magnitude was rare. The sentence reduction was unannounced and was only revealed through an examination of court records. "It's unprecedented," Humberto Dominquez, William's lawyer, conceded in an interview with the Associate Press. "If you go this far, you get these types of rewards. This type of case should set the standard."

William, however, had paid a steep price for his cooperation. He would forever be estranged from his close knit family.

Yet, although none of the other family members agreed to cooperate, they understood William's decision, said Mark Saithes, the Miami lawyer for the family members. But the violent criminal world of Colombia may not be so forgiving. "They would be killed and they know it, in a heartbeat," Dominquez acknowledged. William, his wife and their two daughters were likely candidates for the U.S. Federal Witness Protection Program, Dominquez noted, although their situation could change with time.

So after a thirty-year investigation, Gilberto and Miguel Rodriguez were finally paying for their crimes. The Cali cartel was as dead as Pablo Escobar and his Medellin cartel. Yet did anything really change in the War on Drugs? Gilberto Rodriguez once offered a depressing but prescient take on the cocaine trade. "Economics has a natural law," he declared. "Supply is determined by the demand. When cocaine stops being consumed, when there's no demand for it ... that will be the end of that business."

That end is nowhere in sight, but it is safe to declare that at least two major battles in the War on Drugs has been won: the takedowns of Escobar and the Medellin cartel and that of the Cali cartel. Ironically, the end of what was left of the multinational like Cali cartel, history's most powerful drug trafficking mafia, had come with a whimper, not a bang.

**N**EARLY A DECADE after their convictions, Gilberto and Miguel Rodriguez Orejuela remain incarcerated in American prisons where they will undoubtedly spend the rest of their lives. The cartel they founded is now history. But while Colombia remains an important center in the illegal drug trade, the country today is a far cry from what it was in the 1980s and early 1990s when the War of the Cartels raged. The out-of-control-violence has subsided and the drug trade has diminished in scope.

Remarkably, Medellin has become a tourist center. Yahoo, the web site, has even recommended the city as a destination for American retirees. Today, Pablo Escobar may be even more popular in death than he was while alive. One can even tour a collection of sites relating to El Patrons life. Pablo Escobar may be more popular in death than he was while alive, and his violent and brutal legacy has become a focus of the country's budding tourist trade. Visitors can take what is known as the "Paisa Road Tour" and visit the heavy fortified edifice that was Escobar's base, a shrine on Avenue Pablado the business headquarters of the Medellin cartel and even the Montescaro grayeyard where Pablo is buried.

Another tour ends with a visit to Roberto Escobar's current residence. According to one tourist report, Roberto "openly encouraged our questions, photos and was keen to explain his post cartel pursuits in the medical research field in finding a cure for HIV." One foreign tourist described Roberto—today half blind and half deaf from the letter bomb that went off close to his face—as a gracious host. When Roberto was asked to recall his favorite memory of Pablo, Roberto remembered the time the he escaped prison with his brother.

Roberto claimed that he no longer dwells on that past. "I have repented for everything I've done in my life," he has said. "I have asked Our Father and my mother to forgive me, because I respect my mother a lot. I go to mass and I pray to God every night."

One big question—what happened to the billions of dollars that Escobar made selling heroin to the world? According to Roberto Escobar, "The enemies of my brother and many parts of the Colombian government have taken it." Some believe that Escobar's family may have some of it as well, which, in reality, is small consolation to the Escobars because it has not been easy for the family since the drug kingpin's death. Soon after Pablo's death in 1993, many members tried to flee the country.

The U.S. Embassy reportedly used its influence to deny them safe haven to any country. For instance, Nicholas Escobar, a nephew of Pablo's, and his family fled to Chile, but the U.S. Embassy there pressured the Chilean government to extradite them. The family appealed to the Chilean courts, but the appeal was denied and the family then fled to Germany. When Esocbar's brother Argemiro and his, nephew, sister Luis Maria and her husband and their three children were discovered in Costa Rica, they were deported and flown back to Medellin.

In a remarkable development, Juan Pablo Escobar, one of Pablo's children, has sought atonement for the sins of father Pablo Escobar. For nearly 20 years, the son has been living in Argentina where he changed his name to Sebastian Marroquin. On source said: "If Marroquin grew a mustache, he would be the spitting image of the most famous drug dealer in history."

In 2005, Marroquin was approached by a filmmaker who proposed doing a documentary in which Marroquin would meet with the sons of the Colombian Justice Minister Rodrigo Lara Bonilla and the late presidential candidate Luis Carlos Galan, both of whom were assassinated on Escobar's orders after they challenged him. The result—a riveting documentary in which Marroquin met secretly with the sons on the island in the Rio del Plata, where they sat on a bench and had a "frank but cordial talk."

In the documentary, Marroquin asks his father's victims for their forgiveness. The son of Lara Bonilla replies, "We are both good and peaceful men. Let's move forward." Later in the documentary Marroquin says, "This is very emotional. I hope the Colombian people understand it, and we can help stop the drug violence once and for all."

So what about the big picture—the international drug trade? Did taking down Escobar and the Cali cartel godfathers made any difference? Two decades decade after the U.S. and Colombian law enforcement took down the godfathers from Cali, the DEA regards that victory as perhaps the greatest in the agency's history. Agents also believe the takedown provides an important lesson for those waging the War on Drugs. "At no time can we allow a criminal organization to get as powerful as the Cali cartel did," said Bob Nieves, DEA chief of operations from 1989 to 1995. "The Cali cartel was close to turning Colombia into a narco democracy."

Other sources, however, believe that the takedown of the two big Colombian cartels has made little difference in the War on Drugs. Indeed, their takedowns have provided a wise lesson for other Colombia drug traffickers, namely, becoming too big and complex an organization will make you more vulnerable to a takedown. So today, we see a radically different type of Colombian drug-trafficking organization. Gone is the huge octopus as represented by the Cali cartel, which employed thousands, had a global reach, smuggled large-scale shipments and earned Fortune 500-likerevenues that reached $7 billion annually.

Instead, we have the so-called *cartelitos* or baby cartels, which try to operate as discreetly as the Cali combine did, but do not rely on the sophisticated organizational structure and communications systems that it employed.

"Today's *cartelitos* have learned from the past," explained Pedro M. Guzman, a DEA special agent based in Bogota since 1999. "In the days of the Cali cartel, drug traffickers relied on the cell phone to manage their day-to-day business activities. Today's criminals are using the Internet and push to talk radios as their main means of communication. They sell directly to the Mexicans so the United States won't be able to make extradition cases against them, no matter where the cocaine ends up. They like to have face-to-face meetings, which obviously alleviates the need for micromanaging and the constant need to monitor cell phones in the United States."

This change began in the early 1990s, well before the Rodriguez brothers were captured and their empire began to crumble. By July 1993, an estimated 200 trafficking groups were operating throughout Colombia, at least 100 of which were located in the Cali strongholds of the northern Valle del Cauca area. Six years later, a PBS *Frontline* show reported that "the DEA and Colombian National Police believe there are more than three hundred active drug smuggling organizations."

In another important international development, the Colombians have been willing to cede more control and responsibility to Mexicans in the smuggling of drugs to their biggest market, the United States. This trend began during the Cali era in the early 1990s when law enforcement disrupted the cartel's distribution routes through the Caribbean, and so they turned to their Mexican colleagues to help to move drugs.

Today, the Mexicans, who are paid a fee to move the cocaine across the border, are no longer merely transporters for the Colombians. They now move the drugs to the point of sale and, in return, receive a commission from their Colombian suppliers. "Today, the Mexicans have taken over and are ruling the organized crime and moving the bulk of the money," U.S. drug czar John Walters told the *Christian Science Monitor* in August 2005.

At one time, Colombian drug traffickers were responsible for the 80 to 90 per cent of the cocaine being transported through the U.S, according to Thomas Pietschmann, an analyst with the United Nations Office on Drugs and Crime. "With the takedown of the Cali and Medellin cartels, the Mexican cartels have filled most of the vacuum," he said Pietschmann. "The Mexicans are important on the West Coast and the area right up to the Midwest. Some parts of the East Coast are all that is still controlled by the Colombian cartels."

By 2004, as much as 90 per cent of the cocaine entering the U.S. was being smuggled through Mexican territory, according to the Bureau of International Narcotics and Law Enforcement Affairs. Drugs are flown from Colombia to Mexico, where private vehicles and commercial trucks are used to smuggle them to the U.S. It is impossible to stop every person and every vehicle crossing the border, for at least 48 million pedestrians, 90 million vehicles and 4.4 million trucks cross it annually, according to U.S. Border Patrol estimates.

Some of the most powerful drug lords include Osiel Cardenas (the Gulf cartel), Joaquin "El Chapo" Guzman (Sinaloa cartel), the Arellano Felix family (Tijuana cartel) and Vicente Carrillo Fuentes (Juarez cartel). These drug lords have garnered billions of dollars in profits while corrupting the Mexican political system.

Today Mexico looks like the Colombia of the 1980s and early '90s. In reality, nothing has changed in the War on Drugs, except the players involved in the drug game.

Meanwhile, the war of the cartels that led to the decline of the Colombian cartels is today known as the biggest gang war in history.

ACKNOWLEDGEMENTS

The author has covered The War on Drugs for more than two decades. Thanks to all the sources and professionals who have helped reach the topic during this journey.

Thanks to Dimas Harya and the staffs of Strategic Media Books for their help in publishing this book.

Thanks to my wife Magdalena for her support and encouragement of my writing career. She has played a big part in the journey.

Bowden Mark, *Killing Pablo: The Hunt for the World's Greatest Outlaw*, New York, Penguin Books, 2002

Castillo, Fabio. *Los Jinetes de la Cocaina*. Bogota, Colombia: Documentos Periodisticos, 1988.

Chepesiuk, Ron. Drug Lords, *The Rise and Fall of the Cali Cartel*, London, Milo Books, 2003

*Hard Target: The U.S.'s War on International Drug Trafficking, 1982–1997.* Jefferson, N.C.: McFarland Publishing,1997

*The War on Drugs: An International Encyclopedia.* Santa Barbara, Calif.: ABC-CLIO, 1999

Eddy, Paul, and Hugo Sabogal, and Sara Walden. *The Cocaine Wars,* .New York: W.W. Norton, 1988

Gugliotta, Guy and Jeff Leen, *Kings of Cocaine*, New York, Harper Collins, 1990

Rumpel, William, *At the Devil's Table*, New York, Random House 2011

Strong, Simon, *Whitewash, Pablo Escobar and the Cocaine Wars*, New York, Pan Books, 1995

Ron Chepesiuk is a Rock Hill, SC-based award-winning author of more than 33 books, including *Black Caesar* and *Sergeant Smack*. He is also a Fulbright Scholar, the radio host of the Crime Beat radio show (www.artistfirst.com/crimebeat.htm), a consultant to the History Channel's Gangland TV series and a regular interviewee on U.S. cable TV crime shows.

# CURRENT AND FORTHCOMING TITLES FROM
## STRATEGIC MEDIA BOOKS

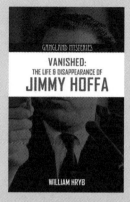

**VANISHED**
The Life and Disappearance of
Jimmy Hoffa

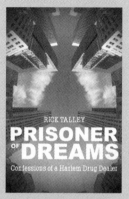

**PRISONER OF DREAMS**
Confessions of
a Harlem Drug Dealer

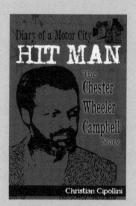

**DIARY OF A MOTOR CITY
HIT MAN**
The Chester
Wheeler Campbell Story

**BLACK CAESAR**
The Rise and Disappearance of
Frank Matthews, Kingpin

## AVAILABLE FROM STRATEGICMEDIABOOKS.COM, AMAZON, AND MAJOR BOOKSTORES NEAR YOU.

COMING IN 2014

### THE SICILIAN MAFIA
A True Crime Travel Guide

### THE GODFATHER OF CRACK:
The True Story of Freeway Ricky Ross

### LUCKY LUCIANO:
Mysterious Tales of a Gangland Legend